T0384193

POLITICAL PHILOSOPHY

This book offers an introduction to political philosophy, the study of the role of government in our lives. It discusses what political philosophy is about, its most important and enduring questions, and how to do political philosophy well. Throughout, the book discusses issues such as:

- Do we have a moral obligation to obey the law?
- What's the value of equality?
- What's the nature of justice?
- How can we answer philosophical questions about politics?
- Is political philosophy a form of activism? Or is it more like a science?

Written in an inviting and accessible style, *Political Philosophy: The Basics* offers an ideal starting point for anyone wishing to learn more about the philosophical study of politics.

Bas van der Vossen is Professor of Philosophy and Associate Director of the Smith Institute of Political Economy and Philosophy at Chapman University, California. He is the co-author of *In Defense of Openness*, with Jason Brennan (2018) and *Debating Humanitarian Intervention,* with Fernando Tesón (2017). He is Associate Editor of *Social Philosophy and Policy*.

THE BASICS

The Basics is a highly successful series of accessible guidebooks which provide an overview of the fundamental principles of a subject area in a jargon-free and undaunting format.

Intended for students approaching a subject for the first time, the books both introduce the essentials of a subject and provide an ideal springboard for further study. With over 50 titles spanning subjects from Artificial Intelligence to Women's Studies, *The Basics* are an ideal starting point for students seeking to understand a subject area.

Each text comes with recommendations for further study and gradually introduces the complexities and nuances within a subject.

CRITICAL THINKING (SECOND EDITION)
Stuart Hanscomb

GLOBAL DEVELOPMENT
Daniel Hammett

FOOD ETHICS (SECOND EDITION)
Ronald Sandler

PERCEPTION
Bence Nanay

PHILOSOPHY OF TIME
Graeme Forbes

CAUSATION
Stuart Glennan

PHILOSOPHY OF LANGUAGE
Ethan Nowak

STOIC ETHICS
Christopher Gill and Brittany Polat

POLITICAL PHILOSOPHY
Bas van der Vossen

Other titles in the series can be found at: https://www.routledge.com/The-Basics/book-series/B

POLITICAL PHILOSOPHY

THE BASICS

Bas van der Vossen

Routledge
Taylor & Francis Group

NEW YORK AND LONDON

Designed cover image: Getty Images

First published 2025
by Routledge
605 Third Avenue, New York, NY 10158

and by Routledge
4 Park Square, Milton Park, Abingdon, Oxon, OX14 4RN

Routledge is an imprint of the Taylor & Francis Group, an informa business

© 2025 Bas van der Vossen

Library of Congress Cataloging-in-Publication Data
Names: Van der Vossen, Bas, 1979- author.
Title: Political philosophy : the basics / Bas van der Vossen.
Description: New York : Routledge, 2024. | Series: The basics |
Includes bibliographical references and index.
Identifiers: LCCN 2024025841 (print) | LCCN 2024025842 (ebook) |
ISBN 9781032168661 (hardback) | ISBN 9781032168654 (paperback) |
ISBN 9781003250692 (ebook)
Subjects: LCSH: Political science—Philosophy. | Political obligation. |
Liberty. | Equality. | Social contract. | Justice. | Activism.
Classification: LCC JA71 .V29 2024 (print) | LCC JA71 (ebook) |
DDC 320.01/1—dc23/eng/20240702
LC record available at https://lccn.loc.gov/2024025841
LC ebook record available at https://lccn.loc.gov/2024025842

ISBN: 978-1-032-16866-1 (hbk)
ISBN: 978-1-032-16865-4 (pbk)
ISBN: 978-1-003-25069-2 (ebk)

DOI: 10.4324/9781003250692

Typeset in Bembo
by codeMantra

CONTENTS

INTRODUCTION

Much of modern philosophy, including political philosophy, starts with the Greek philosopher Socrates (470–399 BCE). In 399 BCE, the city of Athens sentenced Socrates to death on charges of impiety and corrupting the young. Socrates had been going around the city questioning people's values, including the official values of the city. He questioned (and effectively destroyed) religious ideas as well as social and political principles. His uprooting of these ideas made the people of Athens very uncomfortable.

The dialogue *Crito* tells the story of Socrates' last night before his execution[1] (Plato 360 BCE). One of his friends, Crito, visits him in prison and tells Socrates that he and his other friends have arranged an escape. Socrates was innocent, Crito argued, and so the punishment he was about to undergo was clearly unjust. Socrates himself had argued as much in his court case (chronicled by Plato in the *Apology*). Crito offered Socrates a way to save himself and continue the important philosophical work he cared so much about.

But Socrates refused to leave. He wanted to stay and kill himself – by drinking a toxic potion made of hemlock – just as Athens ordered. Socrates thought he couldn't in good conscience disobey the laws of Athens. As he saw it, whenever there's a conflict between the law and your personal opinion

DOI: 10.4324/9781003250692-1

about what's right or wrong, you should follow the law – even if the price is your own life. The dialogue in *Crito* contains Socrates' arguments for this view.

Crito raises several questions, the kind of questions political philosophy deals with. Must we always obey the law? Why do governments have authority over their people? Do they even have authority over people? And who are the people? Why them and not others? What is justice? Is justice determined by the law or is it something else, something independent that we can use to measure whether the law is just or unjust? Do people have rights to things like freedom or fair treatment? And, importantly, how might we actually answer these questions? When we ask these questions, we begin doing political philosophy. Socrates gave arguments for why he thought he should stay in prison and be executed. You might disagree. The question is genuinely difficult.

One reason this question is difficult is that we all have ideas (about politics or other things) that sound plausible on their own, but don't fit together very well. Here's an example. Many people believe something like this is true:

(1)   We should obey the law.

And most would probably also agree that:

(2)   We should not do unjust things.

But if we also think that:

(3)   Socrates' punishment was unjust,

then we face a problem. Because we cannot accept all three claims as true in Socrates' case.

If we accept that (2) and (3) are true – i.e., that Socrates' punishment was indeed unjust and that we really should not do unjust things – then we are committed to the idea that it's permissible for Socrates to escape from prison. But that contradicts (1). Socrates himself thought that (1) was true. But if we are to agree with him, then we must reject either (2) or (3). But both of those statements seem very plausible.

Something is up here. We're dealing with three claims, each of which seems, at first sight, true and important. But we can't accept them all. When we face a situation like this, we may not yet know which claim we should reject, but we know at least one of them has to go. We're about to learn something important: at least one of the political ideas expressed by (1), (2), and (3) is false.

Political philosophy helps us work our way through issues like this. The aim of this book is to help you begin thinking through these types of questions and introduce you to some of the important theories in the field. Hopefully, going through this process of thinking more carefully about politics will make you think that political philosophy is interesting and important. When, finally, you settle on an answer about a particular issue (it can take a while), you should feel like you've made valuable progress. You'll understand the world better, and have a more sophisticated idea about how to approach politics. Few things are more rewarding than that.

NOTE

1 Socrates didn't leave any written works. Much of what we know about him was written down by his student Plato, who wrote several dialogues recounting Socrates' philosophical conversations and arguments.

1

STARTING POLITICAL PHILOSOPHY

The questions Socrates and Crito discuss touch on central issues in political philosophy. Must we, morally speaking, obey the law? What are the conditions under which people have such an obligation? Can governments change what's just and unjust? What, if anything, gives them that authority over their people? Who are "their" people anyway? Are we morally allowed to resist rulers or laws that are unjust? And so on.

These are *political* questions because politics refers to the act of governing, the exercise of authority and control over people in society. Politicians set rules that people are expected to follow, typically in the form of laws. And governments enforce those rules using force or the threat of force, sometimes to the point of death.

These questions are *philosophical* because they involve abstract ideas, such as moral principles or general truths about politics. The word "philosophy" derives from the ancient Greek for love of wisdom, and so political philosophy can be thought of as the search for wisdom about the rules and force used to govern society. Political philosophers ask what kind of governments (if any) might be morally justified, how much coercion they may use, what people are permitted to do when governments overstep their limits, and so on.

When we begin to think about questions like the one Socrates faced, we are starting to do political philosophy. Like

DOI: 10.4324/9781003250692-2

other branches of philosophy, political philosophy tries to understand a part of reality. We're looking for fundamental or general truths that help explain our political world. This chapter looks more closely at how we begin to construct those explanations.

BEGINNING THEORIES

We all engage in philosophical arguments sometimes. Suppose we ask someone, call her Sophia, about Socrates' predicament. Does she think that, morally speaking, Socrates was morally free to escape? Let's say Sophia does think so, believing that Socrates would have done no wrong if he'd chosen to evade his sentence. If we ask Sophia to explain, she will give us her reasons for thinking this. Perhaps she'd say that the punishment was clearly unjust, and no one should be unjustly threatened by their government, or something like that.

In offering her reasons, Sophia begins to construct an argument. We often begin such arguments, even if we don't always follow through on them in a sustained and rigorous manner. Philosophy helps us sort out these ideas, and better understand what they really mean.

Sophia is beginning to think about the relationship between governments and their subjects. And one aspect of this relationship, as she sees it, is that governments shouldn't wrong their subjects. If they do, subjects aren't bound to obey in the same way as they normally would be. At the same time, there are other cases where Sophia does think the government is morally permitted to do things that we don't like. For example, Sophia believes that people should pay their taxes, even when they don't support what the government is doing with the money, or when they think the taxes are too high.

We're faced with a messy bunch of ideas here. And this is quite typical. When we first start thinking about a complicated subject, our thoughts are almost always messy. Still, those initial thoughts are important. They offer the various "observations" from which we build our arguments and our theories, even when the observations might seem to conflict.

To bring some consistency to these ideas, we should take a more detailed look, asking what might explain the discrepancies between them. Often, there will be relevant differences. For instance, Socrates was facing an unjust punishment that threatened his life. That's typically not the case when we need to pay our taxes. Maybe that's relevant: when things start to really get unjust, the moral obligation to obey starts to give way.

Let's use this idea to formulate the following hypothesis about obedience:

> **Sophia's Hypothesis:** We morally ought to obey the law, except when it's unjust.

This hypothesis fits well with Sophia's observations. It allows Socrates to escape, but it doesn't mean we get to evade our taxes all the time.

Note what we've been doing. Sophia began by rejecting Socrates' claim that we should always obey the law. But looking at her other ideas, we discovered that she doesn't think we *never* have to obey when we disagree with a law. The issue looked pretty messy and complicated, but when we looked a little closer, we were able to formulate a hypothesis that brought some order to these ideas. This is the start of building a philosophical theory.

BUILDING THEORIES

A hypothesis is not a theory. But it is an important step toward one. Sophia's hypothesis gives coherence to her observations, but it does not yet explain *why* those observations are the way they are (or the way she thinks they are). A theory helps us understand that. It doesn't just tell us *how* things are, it tells us *why* they are that way.

When Socrates refused Crito's offer to escape, he invoked a principle that explained his refusal. Here is how Socrates saw things:[1]

> He who has experience of the manner in which we order justice and administer the State, and still remains, has entered into an implied contract that he will do as we [i.e., the laws] command him.
>
> (Plato 360 BCE)

Socrates spent his life in Athens. And, to him, this meant that he agreed to obey its laws. Socrates imagined the laws of Athens speaking to him, and explaining why it would be wrong to escape now. The reason is that he, Socrates,

> has made an agreement with us that he will duly obey our commands; and he neither obeys them nor convinces us that our commands are wrong; and we do not rudely impose them, but give him the alternative of obeying or convincing us; that is what we offer and he does neither.
>
> (Plato 360 BCE)

The reason to obey the law, then, is that Socrates chose to live in Athens, even though he could have left. Choosing to continue to live in Athens is the same as agreeing to obey the law of Athens, and you should keep your word. You don't get to break your promises just because you don't like doing what you promised. For that reason, Socrates thinks he should obey the law and kill himself.

This gets us closer to a theory. We can summarize it roughly as follows:

> **Socrates' Theory:** When you live in a place for a long time, you thereby agree to obey its laws. And if you agree to do something, you are morally required to do it.

This theory explains why Socrates saw things as he did. It's not a given that he should obey. There's a reason: through his past actions, Socrates agreed to do so.

Theories are useful because they offer general explanations for certain observations. These explanations help us understand both why things are the way they are, and how things might be in cases other than the one we're thinking about now. Socrates' theory performs pretty well in this respect. If true, it explains not only why he ought to obey the laws of Athens, but also what your or my position might be with respect to the laws we face.

Sophia thought Socrates' conclusion was wrong. And so (unless Socrates' argument convinced her otherwise), she'll have to reject this theory, too. Better still, she may come up with a different, and better, theory of her own. Perhaps Sophia doesn't believe that living in a place means you agree to follow its laws. Or perhaps she does agree with that part, but not that agreeing to follow its laws means you must follow *all* its laws. Take the latter idea. We might formulate something like the following rival theory:

> **Sophia's Rival Theory:** When you live in a place for a long time, you thereby agree to obey the laws of that place that are not seriously unjust. And if you agree to do something, you are morally required to do it.

This theory is also pretty good. It explains why we should obey the law in many cases, like when paying taxes or following restaurant hygiene codes. It explains why Socrates might be free to disobey. And we can also use it to think about different circumstances, including our own.

We now have two theories that conflict. Socrates' theory says he must drink the hemlock. Sophia's says he's free to escape. Both cannot be right at the same time. We need a way to figure out what's correct here.[2]

TESTING THEORIES

Theories are supposed to help us better understand things. We begin with a bunch of messy, unordered ideas and observations, and then construct a theory to figure out how they fit together. In this sense, philosophers are a bit like scientists. We use theories to explain parts of reality and use our observations as inputs for those theories. The goal is to formulate principles or general truths that best explain those inputs. A good theory identifies such principles or truths, and relates them to reality in a way that helps us understand things better.

The test of a theory, then, is how well it performs this task. Does it correctly explain reality, or at least explain it better than other available theories? Think of our initial ideas and observations as data points, and of a theory as providing a way to explain those data points. A theory will look better when it explains more points, and especially if explains more important ones. It will also look better if the explanation it offers is powerful and plausible.

More precisely, we can evaluate theories by looking at three things. (There are other ways we can evaluate theories, too, but these three are particularly important.) They're listed here in no particular order, and it's perfectly possible for a theory to be attractive even though it doesn't perform especially well on one of these.

(1) *Explanatory power.* A theory has explanatory power when it offers a useful description of what causes certain phenomena. In the case of Socrates, the phenomenon in question is that he was (purportedly) not morally free to escape. Socrates' theory identifies the cause of this to be his previous actions, which Socrates thought made him bound to stay. The explanatory power of his theory depends on whether remaining in Athens is a relevant cause of an obligation to obey its laws.

(2)   *Plausibility.* Theories are built around central claims or principles. Theories become more attractive to the extent that
these claims or principles are plausible. The plausibility of
principles depends on whether we can see them clearly at
play in a variety of contexts, and on whether they're generally accepted, have weird exceptions, are ideologically
slanted, are impartial or self-serving, and so on.

(3)   *Fit with observations.* The central principles of theories
have implications for how we should think about particular cases. Such principles are attractive when they fit
more of the initial observations that we start with, and
especially when they fit ones we have a lot of confidence
in. The more a theory yields correct answers in these
cases, the more attractive it becomes.

Consider again our two theories. Socrates claimed he was
morally bound to stay. His theory offers an adequate explanation for this conclusion, as it bases it on the idea that Socrates
had agreed to obey the law, and that agreements can bind us
to do things. Moreover, this explanation is pretty plausible. It's
a very familiar thought that our agreements can bind us –
something we encounter on a daily basis, and readily take for
granted. We even accept this when we have to do things that
we don't want to do. And Socrates' claim that being somewhere means you agree to follow the rules is also plausible.
Again, this is something we run into quite frequently. If I visit
your home, I should follow your rules.

So, on the first two dimensions, Socrates' theory performs
well. It offers a useful explanation for the obligation to obey the
law, and this explanation is plausible. However, the theory fal-
ters somewhat on the third count, fit with observations. Socrates' theory implies that we ought to obey *all* the laws of whatever
place we happen to live in, and that does not seem to fit some
of our initial observations. As we observed with Sophia, it's easy
to disagree with Socrates here, and many people indeed do.

This objection can be strengthened, as there are other cases
where Socrates' theory is also problematic. Suppose, for

example, that our government requires that you perform some racist act. Say you have a restaurant and the law prohibits you from serving Black people at the counter. Would it be *wrong* to refuse to comply? Socrates' theory implies that the answer is yes, but that seems false. At least as long as disobedience wouldn't have some terrible side effects (like sparking riots or whatever), you would do no wrong by resisting this injustice. (It might even be wrong not to resist.)

Sophia's rival theory performs much better here. It avoids these problems by allowing you to disobey unjust laws. That fits our starting observations better. However, Sophia's rival theory has its own drawbacks. Most importantly, it lacks explanatory power. In fact, Sophia's theory doesn't really offer much of an explanation at all. Her theory simply added some exceptions to Socrates' view. But Socrates' theory doesn't explain those exceptions (after all, he denied that they exist), and so we're left without understanding why Sophia thinks we may sometimes disobey. Nor can we predict what Sophia's theory would say in other cases.

If our initial observations are like data points, dots scattered on a graph, we can think of theories as drawing trendlines. These lines will connect a bunch of those points, explaining the relation between them. A clear theory organized around a plausible principle produces a regular and predictable trend-line. That line not only connects various points, but it can also be extended to places where we have fewer or no observations. This makes it useful for thinking about what to do in other situations – we can extrapolate the theory's predictions.

At the same time, such a theory will rarely connect *all* our initial observations. It will connect some points on our graph, it will come very close but not quite connect others, and it may be quite far away from still others. These will be initial observations that clash with the principle around which the theory is organized. If we really believe in the theory, those observations will need to be rejected as outliers (because they clash with the theory). That may include some observations in which we initially had a good amount of confidence.

Socrates' theory roughly behaves like that. It's built around a clear and straightforward principle, which explains many of our initial ideas quite well. It's useful for understanding other cases, too, as it offers clear predictions. However, it runs into problems when it clashes with some of our initial observations. The idea that we must obey the law, come what may, seems too demanding and, in some cases, simply false.

Sophia's rival theory connects more dots. It might even connect all the dots we really care about. But the theory she proposes is not as clear or easy to use. Using the metaphor of the trendline again, the line she proposes is not as regular. It jumps from point to point, wherever these may be on our graph. While it will have few or no cases where it yields the *wrong* answers, this theory has much less explanatory power. We don't know why the dots are connected, and we can't really know how to extend this theory to cases we haven't encountered yet.

In the end, the choice between theories depends on which offers the best *overall* package of explanation, plausibility, and fit. That may be Socrates' theory, it may be Sophia's rival theory – it may be some third theory. Regardless, we'd have some interesting work ahead of us. If Socrates' theory is correct, we have to revise several of our initial ideas – including, but not limited to, the idea that we can disobey or resist unjust regimes. And if we truly can't disobey or resist, we need to ask what our position with respect to such laws really is. If Sophia's rival theory is true, we need to ask why it is true. We want to know why we can disobey in some cases but not others. And we want to know whether this permission to disobey translates to other situations as well.

REFLECTIVE EQUILIBRIUM

Testing theories involves a kind of back and forth. We begin with some ideas and questions, and then use these to formulate a rough theory. We then test that theory by seeing how it matches with what, when we really consider it, we think is true. If the theory clashes with our initial ideas, we need to choose between it and those ideas. Sometimes, the best thing is to keep the theory and give up on the ideas. Sometimes, the best thing is to revise or give up on the theory. In the end, we're looking for the best attainable balance between ideas we think true and principles we find compelling.

Socrates' theory said the following.

> **Socrates' Theory**: When you live in a place for a long time, you thereby agree to obey its laws. And if you agree to do something, you are morally required to do it.

Three elements are present here:

(1)   A general principle that if you agree to do something, you morally ought to do it.
(2)   An application of that principle, saying that if you live someplace for a long time, that's the same as agreeing to follow its laws.
(3)   An implication of that principle, saying that if you agree to obey the law, you must even do things like carrying out unjust punishments or killing yourself.

We imagined Sophia worrying about the third element. Socrates' situation seems pretty extreme, but other examples like having to support racist practices are maybe even more worrisome. It doesn't seem right that we can make it morally *wrong* to refuse to participate in racism and injustice, simply by agreeing to follow the rules of society. Saying that clashes with some initial ideas of Sophia, ideas that are pretty widely shared, plausible, and aren't ideologically slanted or self-serving.

Sophia proposed that we make the third element less strict, to say that our agreements don't bind us to just anything, but only to things that are not unjust. But we cannot simply change that element by itself. Because (3) is said to be an implication of (1), if we change (3), then we must change (1) along with it.

Sophia's rival theory, then, must look something like this:[3]

(1') A general principle that if you agree to do something, you morally ought to do it, as long as it's not seriously unjust.

(2') An application of that principle, saying that if you live someplace for a long time, that's the same as agreeing to follow its laws.

(3') An implication of that principle, saying that if you agree to obey the law, you must do so, as long as it's not seriously unjust.

Is there good reason for accepting (1') instead of (1)? Here's one possible reason. Agreements are like contracts, transferring something we have to someone else. In the case of Socrates, he transferred *a right* – specifically, he transferred the right to choose how he acts to Athens. That's how Athens got the right that Socrates obey its laws in the first place. The city didn't start out with that right. But it received that right from Socrates as a result of his agreement, stated in (2) and (2').

However, we cannot transfer things we don't own. I cannot sell you my neighbor's car, for example. It's simply not mine to sell. So, even if we come to some kind of "agreement" about it, and you pay me money, you still don't become the owner of the car. Whatever we did, it wasn't a sale, and the reason is simple: I didn't own the thing I was pretending to sell.

Something similar applies here. We don't have a right, the argument goes, to do unjust things. As so we cannot transfer this right to others either. We cannot bind ourselves to do unjust things through agreeing. The upshot is that when Socrates transferred to Athens the right to tell him how to live, he didn't give it the right to order him to do something that's unjust. He couldn't have given that right to Athens, since Socrates never had that right to begin with. If Athens ordered him to do racist things, he would not have to obey. Similarly, if

Athens ordered him to an unjust death, he would not have to obey.

Here we have an argument for why (1') may be true.[4] If the argument is correct, it provides an explanation for Sophia's alternative principle. Note the back and forth. We began with a theory that says Socrates should drink the hemlock. That theory conflicts with some important initial observations, such as the idea that we don't have to commit injustices just because our government says so. We went back to the theory to see if there might be a reason for amending it in a way that makes its conclusions more plausible. The idea that we cannot bind ourselves to do unjust things is such a reason. If true, Sophia's rival theory could outperform Socrates' theory. It offers more plausible conclusions, based on a plausible explanation.

The back and forth can continue, of course. Not everyone accepts the explanation that we cannot bind ourselves to commit injustice. Some people who object to this explanation worry, for instance, that it may be dangerous if everyone starts second-guessing whether the law is just. Without a clear obligation to obey all laws, society may start to fall apart, they fear. This objection might lead to further changes to the theory, possibly leading to an even more sophisticated view. Or maybe this is the point where we find we simply have to choose: accept Sophia's rival theory, with its dangers in tow, or accept that Socrates was right after all.

Building philosophical theories involves lots of theoretical adjustments like this. We begin to formulate a theory, give up on some of our initial beliefs, tweak the theory when we realize that it still clashes with some important truths, test it again, and so on. After a while, we'll arrive at a point where we think the best trade-off between good results and good principles has been achieved. That point is often called *reflective equilibrium*.[5]

Reflective equilibrium is the point at which there's a balance between the initial ideas that we can continue to accept as correct, and the principles that we accept as true. It's the place at which there is no further useful back and forth. The theory we identify in reflective equilibrium may still have some unappealing features. It may not explain certain initial ideas, it may imply that certain things are true that we initially thought had to be false, it may mean we should reject principles we thought were true or must accept principles we first thought suspect. Nevertheless, once we find this balance, changing the theory will make it worse – sacrificing too much plausibility, say, or bringing along too many strange implications. On balance, it will be the best theory we can get.

LOCAL VERSUS GLOBAL CONSISTENCY

One reason philosophy is important is that we often have beliefs that are not well founded. Socrates thought he had to drink the hemlock because he'd agreed to obey the law. But that inference seems to be wrong. Agreeing to obey the law arguably doesn't bind you to do unjust things, and so even though Socrates lived his entire life in Athens, that did not imply an agreement to drink the hemlock.

Another reason philosophy is important is that we sometimes have contradictory beliefs. We might think that we cannot agree to do unjust things, but also think that it's unacceptable for people to disobey the law whenever they think it unjust. Those beliefs may turn out to be contradictory (although whether they *really* are is a further philosophical question). If they are contradictory, we can't continue to accept both – we'll need to choose. By doing so, we'll learn that one of the ideas we began with, and that initially seemed important and true, must be rejected upon reflection.

Philosophy helps us filter out these kinds of mistakes from our thinking. Through philosophical deliberation, our ideas become more logical and less contradictory, slowly but surely. Our thinking becomes more *consistent*, and we're beginning to understand the world better. At the same time, the more we do philosophy, the more we start realizing just how much our initial ideas are messy and unorganized. This can be almost overwhelming, knowing that we have so many ideas – even just ideas about politics – but don't know exactly how they're all supposed to fit together.

Even when we figure out what to think about Socrates' plight, we still may have little idea what to think, say, about economic inequality, abortion, or immigration. Nor will we have much grasp on whether there are any connections between these questions. Does saying one thing about Socrates commit us to taking a position on these other issues? That happens more often than you might think, but it also can be difficult to see what the implications might be. Only by doing careful philosophical thinking can we determine the connections.

Let's call it "local consistency" when we achieve consistency in one part of our thinking. Achieving local consistency doesn't mean achieving consistency in all our thinking – we can call that "global consistency." In fact, sometimes, achieving local consistency can *decrease* our global consistency. This happens when smoothing our thinking about one issue, say, about the obligation to obey the law, involves accepting things that conflict with some of our other beliefs. We may or may not be aware of it, but it can happen easily.

All of that is okay. Trying to force *all* of our thoughts into one consistent whole is probably not desirable. Life is complicated, full of different values and commitments and principles. We care about equality, freedom, respect, justice, prosperity, community. All of those things matter, in some way, shape, or form, even if our initial thinking about them is a mess. It's important to think about how these ideas fit together, what they really mean, and what they demand of us. But it's also important not to lose sight of their importance just because we can't always fully figure out how they relate to one another.

One easy way to achieve global consistency is to simplify reality, reducing all our initial ideas to implications of one simple theory. Such a simple theory may provide answers to all possible questions in a neat and consistent manner. But all too often, that theory also ends up being overly simplistic, or even ridiculous. It will look elegant because it crammed all the mess into a consistent whole. But it will also be false because this cramming involved doing violence to lots of things that matter. We'll be forced to simply abandon too many ideas that are true and important.

The key to good philosophy is doing both things at the same time. We want to bring consistency to our thinking, starting locally and slowly working our way outward. And we want to do this without losing sight of the many and complicated things that really matter in life. Doing this will probably mean we have to continue to live with a good deal of *inconsistency*, simply because we don't have the time, energy, or brainpower to figure out how everything that matters actually fits together.[6]

The best we can do, then, is strive for *more* consistency, overall. By starting with questions like the one Socrates faced, we can make sense of our ideas and work our way out. We'll be asking whether these ideas fit together, whether they have implications for other issues, and whether those implications can be squared with our thinking about the initial topic. Sometimes, we'll need to go back again and adjust some more. Sometimes, we'll have to accept that this is the best overall view we can construct. And so on. Slowly but certainly, our thinking will bring more consistency and reason to our world-view. Succeeding in this, even only to a degree over one's lifetime, is a very nice achievement indeed.

QUESTIONS

(1) What's the difference between a theory and an argument? When would you find use for one or the other?

(2) Sometimes we feel we can answer a question. Sometimes we feel like we need a theory before we can answer. What accounts for the difference between these two situations?

(3) Suppose you have reached reflective equilibrium. Suppose I have also reached it. Now suppose we still disagree. How can we solve that disagreement? Do we need to?

NOTES

1 In fact, this is just one among several reasons Socrates offers for refusing Crito's offer.

2 Of course, it may turn out that both theories are wrong, and some third theory is correct.

3 The argument's steps here are numbered with primes to indicate that these are revisions of the earlier argument's claims.

4 This is a quick summary of an argument I offer in much more detail in Van der Vossen (2021).

5 The term comes from John Rawls (Rawls 1999 [1971]).

6 Some inconsistency may even be unavoidable, no matter how much brainpower you're packing. Most theories are inaccurate to some degree. They have to simplify reality, reducing it to a general principle or set of rules that we think important or significant. But this reduction inevitably leaves out relevant or even important facts or details. If theories weren't inaccurate in this way, they would not be theories anymore but simply one-to-one descriptions or mirrors of reality. Think of a map. A map that doesn't simplify reality at all would have to be the same size as the real world it depicts. Such a map would be useless.

POLITICAL OBLIGATION

The dialogue in *Crito* discusses whether Socrates ought to obey the law, even though the price is death. This is called the question of political obligation, and it remains a central question in political philosophy. This question is not about whether we're *legally* obligated to obey the law. That's easy to answer. As a matter of the law itself, of course we're required to obey. That's what the law is for, to bind us to do things. What Socrates and Crito were discussing is whether, *morally* speaking, we should do what the law says.

Political obligation is closely related to the question of authority. If people are obligated to obey, that gives governments and officials the right to rule. This right would then be a moral right, a right that is "correlated" to that obligation.[1] If people have political obligations, then the authorities are owed obedience by the people. Governments that have a right to rule can be called legitimate. Governments that lack it, illegitimate. This chapter discusses some of the central ideas and theories surrounding political authority and obedience.

THE QUESTION

When you're obligated to obey, you ought to do what the law says. Of course, there are many instances where morally speaking, we should do what the law says anyway. The law requires

DOI: 10.4324/9781003250692-3

you to not commit murder, and that's certainly something you shouldn't do. But really, you shouldn't do that anyway, so the law doesn't really make a difference here.

Political obligation is the requirement to do what the law says *because* the law says so. You should do what the law says, even if you would otherwise have no reason for it. It may be morally fine to sell a beer to a 20-year-old. But if you're in the US, political obligation means it's wrong to do so. Of course, you might get away with it, and you might not cause any harm by doing it. But you'd be doing something morally wrong, nonetheless. You'd be breaking your political obligation.

Political obligation gives people authority over others. Authority is the power to decide what people must do (as if you're the "author" of their actions), by making actions right or wrong. Ordinarily, people don't have that kind of power over others. I cannot make trivial things morally wrong or required for you. And I can't change things that are wrong into things that are right. Yet our governments purport to have this power. The question of political obligation is whether and to what extent they do.

Few people think we're better off without any government. Without a government, we would lack an organized police force, a single authoritative legal code, a national defense system, and so on. Things might get very hectic, and life quite a bit worse. But that is not enough to answer the question of political obligation – why governments have authority over their subjects. Crito might accept all these points. He's not saying that we should dismantle the state. He's asking whether we should always do what that state tells us, just because it's the law.

A good justification for political obligation and authority has to reflect the fact that people aren't born subject to others. We don't have natural authority over others: I'm not the boss of you, and you're not the boss of me, at least not without good reason. To justify political obligation and establish that authority is legitimate, we have to show that there *is* good reason. We have to show that there is enough reason for some people to be in charge of others.

THE CONSENT OF THE GOVERNED

Socrates said that he'd agreed to obey the laws of Athens (by living there). This has come to be known as the *consent theory* of political obligation. It sees political obligation as grounded in agreement. Legitimate authorities rule with the consent of the people, and the people are obligated to obey because they agreed to do so.

The idea is perhaps most famously expressed in the Preamble of the United States' Declaration of Independence:

> We hold these truths to be self-evident, that all men are created equal, that they are endowed by their Creator with certain unalienable Rights, that among these are Life, Liberty and the pursuit of Happiness. That to secure these rights, Governments are instituted among Men, deriving their just powers from the consent of the governed.

Socrates' argument for this idea[2] was rather short. A more detailed version was offered by the English philosopher John Locke (1632–1704), whose work was the inspiration for the passage just quoted. In the *Second Treatise of Government*, Locke argued that legitimate authority can only be created through people's voluntary consent (Locke 1988 [1689]). Locke's starting point is that people are naturally free and equal. For Locke, this means that we can become subject to the will of others only as a result of our own actions. The primary way we can do this is by freely giving consent.

Locke's argument is based on a commonsense idea: things that are wrongful in the absence of consent can become okay if we do them with permission. It's wrong, for example, for people to cut into your body with sharp objects. But if you consent to undergo surgery, a doctor may do this. This is not because the world is better with doctors around. Nor is the reason that they're somehow special, or that you need surgery, or some such thing. The reason is simple: you gave them permission. If you withdraw your permission, even the best doctor in the world is not allowed to cut into you, no matter how much you need surgery.

Locke sees political authority the same way. No one gets to decide for others how they must live, but governments claim to have just that right. The only way they can have that right is by getting it from the people. Legitimate governments, that is, receive their authority to govern from the consent of the governed. Governments that rule without consent are illegitimate, and they're illegitimate precisely because they don't receive consent.[3]

Locke uses this argument to great effect in his attack on governments that claim absolute power. Since all the rights governments possess are given to it by the people, no government can truly claim rights that we would never freely give up. The right to wield absolute power is such a right. Since we didn't give our governments that right (no sensible person would ever give up such a right), government can't truthfully claim absolute power over their people without losing legitimacy. Absolute rulers are tyrannical, Locke argues, since tyranny by definition is the exercise of power beyond right (Locke 1988 [1689]: Second Treatise, section 199).[4]

Consent, according to Locke, can be given in one of two ways. The first is "express consent", explicitly agreeing to obey the law. The second is "tacit consent," meaning consent given without explicitly saying so. Express consent is familiar. It's what happens when we make a promise to obey, such as when immigrants take an oath of allegiance upon acquiring citizenship. Tacit consent refers to something else. Locke has in mind agreements we make through our (other) actions. We can agree to things, Locke thinks, even when we don't actually sign on the dotted line or say "I agree." When you go to a restaurant and order food, you can't escape the bill by saying you never agreed to pay. The action of sitting down and ordering off the menu means you agree to pay. That agreement happened "tacitly," but it happened nonetheless.

Locke, like Socrates, thought that living in a country means agreeing to obey in this tacit manner. As Locke writes:

> [E]very man, that hath any Possessions, or Enjoyment, of any part of the Dominions of any Government, doth thereby give his *tacit Consent*, and is as far forth obliged to Obedience to the Laws of that Government, during such Enjoyment, as any one under it; whether this his Possession be of Land, to him and his Heirs for ever, or a Lodging only for a Week; or whether it be barely travelling freely on the Highway; and in Effect, it reaches as far as the very being of any one within the Territories of that Government.
>
> (Locke 1988 [1689]: II, 119)

This is known as the *consent theory of political obligation*, and it has several attractive features. For one, it draws on familiar ideas. We all know that our agreements can give people rights they otherwise wouldn't have. When we agree to obey someone else's rules, we thereby obligate ourselves to obey those rules. That gives them the right to tell us what to do. We also know that we can agree to do things without using words. Ordering food in a restaurant is one example, but there are many others. Theorists like Locke and Socrates claim that living somewhere is similar, an agreement to do something without using words.

Second, the theory sees governments as beholden to the people. We do not live to serve the state; the state is here to serve us. That's why we agree to obey in the first place, and it's part of the deal that the government will continue to be of service. Whatever agreement we make when we consent to obey the law, then, it's part of the deal that governments will respect the limits of their proper authority. When regimes overstep those limits, disobedience does not involve *us* breaking our agreement. It's the government who went beyond what was agreed to in the first place. Obedience to that kind of rule was never part of the deal.

The third reason the consent theory is attractive is that a happy conclusion is in the offing. Locke and Socrates both argue that everyone in society agrees to obey the law. That means our governments are legitimate, and we can expect everyone to follow their rules. The key idea here is that residing in a society is equivalent to explicitly agreeing to follow the rules. Since clearly not everyone in society has "expressly" agreed to obey the law, the theory of "tacit" consent is needed.

A DILEMMA FOR CONSENT THEORY

Here is the argument proposed by Socrates, a variant of which Locke worked out in more detail:

(1) Socrates could have left Athens, but freely chose to live there.
(2) If you freely choose to live somewhere, you agree to obey that society's laws.
(3) Therefore, Socrates agreed to obey the laws of Athens.
(4) If you agreed to do something, you're morally obligated to do it.
(5) Therefore, Socrates had a moral obligation to obey the laws of Athens.

Arguments like this represent an inference from premises to (one or more) conclusions. This particular argument contains three premises – the statements (1), (2), and (4) – and two conclusions – the intermediate conclusion in (3), which follows from the first two premises, and the conclusion in (5), which follows from that intermediate conclusion and statement (4). When logically valid, the premises of an argument *entail* the conclusion, meaning that the conclusion must be true if the premises are all true. In other words, if (1), (2), and

(4) are true, then (5) *must* also be true. An argument that's valid and whose premises are all true is called sound.

The argument above is logically valid; there are no inferential gaps. Are the premises true? Premise (1) simply states a fact about Socrates' life. Premise (2) expresses Locke's idea of tacit consent, that by living somewhere you agree to obey the law. And premise (4) states the ethical principle that agreements can create obligations. Since it's hard to deny (4) – it's something we rely on basically every day – the real question is whether (2) is true.

Does his staying in Athens really mean that Socrates agreed to obey its laws? On the face of it, this idea is very intuitive. Clearly, it's true that when I stay in your home, I have to obey your rules. So, isn't it then also true that if I stay in a society, I should obey its rules? When we visit other countries, we feel like we should obey their rules, too. So surely the same is true at home.

Despite being intuitive, this idea has faced strong opposition. Most famously, Scottish philosopher David Hume (1711–1776) denied it was true. In his essay "Of the Original Contract," Hume argued against the consent theory, and one of his objections was that the idea of tacit consent is problematic. Hume asked:

> Can we seriously say, that a poor peasant or artizan has a free choice to leave his country, when he knows no foreign language or manners, and lives from day to day, by the small wages which he acquires? We may as well assert, that man, by remaining in a vessel, freely consents to the dominion of the master; though he was carried on board while asleep, and must leap into the ocean, and perish, the moment he leaves her.
>
> (Hume 1987 [1752]: 475)

Hume agreed that we can create obligations via consent. But he emphasized that consent works only if it's given freely. In this passage, he denies that growing up and living in a society means that you freely consent to follow its rules. Or at least, it doesn't mean that for everyone. If Hume is correct, premise (2) in the argument above is false, and we don't have to accept the consent theory's conclusion.[5]

Hume's point creates a dilemma for consent theory. On the one hand, consent theorists can say that consent really must be given freely. In that case, it may be true – as Hume insisted – that only some people have given government their consent. But this really threatens the ability of consent theory to show that our governments are legitimate, that they have the right to rule over all the people they govern. Here is an argument why that's the case:

(1) Not everyone who lives under a government freely consents to that government (Hume's point in the quotation above).
(2) If someone didn't freely consent, then they have no consent-based political obligations.
(3) Therefore, not everyone who lives under a government has consent-based political obligations.
(4) A government's right to rule is correlated to people's political obligations.
(5) Therefore, governments do not have a consent-based right to rule over everyone who lives under them.
(6) Governments are legitimate only if they have a right to rule over everyone they govern.
(7) Therefore, governments lack consent-based legitimacy.

This horn of the dilemma considerably undercuts the consent theory's appeal. One of the attractions of consent theory was that it could show why our governments are legitimate. If Hume is correct, then it fails to do so.

The other horn of the dilemma would be for consent theory to weaken the requirements for successful consent. Perhaps consent does not have to be given freely, or at least not *so* freely as to rule out the peasants and artisans from Hume's story. But this is no easy solution either. The point that consent must be freely given is not something Hume just came up with, something to pin on the theory in order to reject it. The idea is absolutely central to the view. Consent theory purports to show that governments can be legitimate, even though no one naturally has authority over anyone else. It does this by showing that people have (allegedly) freely imposed government on themselves. Since we can't really complain about things we impose on ourselves, this would do the trick – it would make governments legitimate.

Neither horn of the dilemma is particularly attractive for consent theory, then. And this represents a big problem for the view. Hume's objection strikes at the heart of the theory. Whichever option we choose, we have to let go of the idea that governments rule with the consent of the people simply because they live there.

DEMOCRACY

There are other ways in which people have tried to connect the idea of living and participating in society with consent. One common proposal is to focus on democratic elections. Democratic governments, it's said, are based on consent because people get to vote. And through their voting, people give consent. Democracies thus rule with the consent of the governed, and this gives them a unique kind of legitimacy.

This is a popular argument, but it runs into some powerful objections. Most importantly, it overlooks an important distinction between two kinds of legitimacy, each of which requires a different kind of consent. One is the legitimacy of a specific government or regime. This kind of legitimacy is often related to the way governments come into power. Peaceful transitions, and especially transitions that happen with the support of the people, can confer this kind of legitimacy on a government. When a government wins an election, we can say that they are legitimately in power. If their opponents were to seize power instead, that government would be illegitimate.

That's one kind of legitimacy. But so far, we have been concerned with another kind – the legitimacy of the *state*, and its governing more broadly. This second kind of legitimacy concerns whether a state, the institution that's controlled by specific governments, can rightfully claim to be in charge of people. There's an important difference between these two legitimacy questions. One is about a government that's running the apparatus of the state. The other is about the state itself, irrespective of which government might be in charge at a given time.

Answering one of these questions does not offer an answer to the other. Asking whether a government came into power legitimately is different from asking whether the state as such can legitimately rule over people. Even if a specific government that controls the state is not legitimate, it may still be true that the state as such is legitimate. Election fraud, for example, can put an illegitimate government in charge of what's otherwise a legitimate state. Here, the rule of the state is in principle justifiable, but the government controlling that state is not rightfully in charge.

Conversely, a government may come into power through the best possible means, yet the rule by this particular state (the state that this government controls) remains illegitimate. For example, when Indian people objected to English rule over India and sought independence, their objection wasn't to the fairness of English elections. Their objections were not that this or that government wasn't rightfully in charge of the English state. Their objections were simply that the English state had no right to rule over India at all. No matter how fair their elections might be, the fact that the English were ruling over Indian society rendered that rule illegitimate. This is the second kind of legitimacy, the legitimacy of the state.[6]

Theories of political obligation are concerned with this second kind of (state) legitimacy.[7] They're asking whether people are morally bound to obey the authorities, whether those authorities have a right to rule over people. Democratic elections cannot confer this broader, more fundamental legitimacy. Even if an election was stolen, that doesn't mean the law loses all of its binding force. Elections aren't about that. They're not about whether there should be a government at all, or even whether some other country should be in charge. (You can't vote for the Canadian government in a US election.) They're about who, specifically, should be running the state that's in place.

This is not to say anything bad about democracy. It's far better to live in a democracy than not. Democracies are safer, richer, and more peaceful. But that's not really in question here. Our question is whether voting counts as consent to being governed in the first place. And that question must be answered no. We can see this pretty easily by thinking about people who don't vote. You might hear that they've lost their right to complain, or something like that. But you never hear that they don't have to obey the law because they didn't vote and so didn't agree to it.[8]

Upon reflection, this is no great surprise. A lot of important political questions have to be settled before we can even show up to vote. Democratic elections require rules about how they're to be structured – whether to use proportional representation, first-past-the-post, some kind of weighted ballot, or something else. They require rules about which offices are up for election, what their powers will be, and much, much more. Those questions have to be settled before we can have an election. After all, when we vote, we need to know what we're voting for.

You may be losing your faith in the consent theory of political obligation at this point. If even the consent of democratic elections can't establish state legitimacy, is there any way a state can receive the consent that's needed? Most likely, the answer is no. But that raises a further question. If governments can't really claim to have been *given* their powers by (all) their people, does that matter?

It did to Locke. For Locke, government can be legitimate only if it's adopted *voluntarily*. To him, that's what makes a country free, that the people freely accept their government. But we saw Hume point out that this is just not going to happen fully. Even if some people, even if many people, freely accept being ruled, there will always be people who do not accept it. But the states and the governments that run them don't care, of course. They don't let you opt out. They don't even ask if you'd like to opt out. They may let you leave, but then you'd have to accept some other government elsewhere.

In this sense, states are coercive. They impose themselves on people without their consent, and that includes democratic governments. This means we're at a crossroads. One road involves holding fast to the Lockean idea of a free society. But that idea may mean that our governments are probably not legitimate, or at least not legitimate for all of us. The other road involves rethinking our ideas about legitimacy, and possibly giving up on the idea that subjection to government must be voluntary in order to be legitimate. If Locke's theory gets in trouble because he wants government to be voluntarily adopted, perhaps that's a mistake? Perhaps we should think about government in a different, non-voluntary way.

NATURALISM

Many theories of political obligation indeed reject this voluntarism, the idea that legitimate authority must be freely accepted. They see membership in political society as not really being a choice. Typically, they reject voluntarism precisely because it makes it hard to establish that *everyone* must obey the law. This desire to show that governments have the right to rule us all has made philosophers look for alternative, non-voluntary justifications. These come in different flavors. Some say that we all *benefit* from being governed, and that means we are subordinate to the government. Others say we cannot have *justice* without a government, and that means we must obey.[9] And so on.

Perhaps the oldest version of a *non-voluntaristic* theory of political obligation is called *political naturalism*. Most famously, this theory is defended by the Greek philosopher Aristotle (384–322 BCE) in Book I of the *Politics* (Aristotle 2014). This theory holds membership in society and rule by government to be natural facts, things we're not free to escape. We're born into society, this argument goes, and the obligation to obey the law simply is part of that.

We can summarize this as follows:

(1)   People are naturally members of political society.
(2)   If you're a member of a society, you morally ought to obey its laws.
(3)   Therefore, people morally ought to obey the laws of their society.

Aristotle defended the first premise in several ways. One reason he offers is that people cannot be self-sufficient living apart from society. Only the state can be self-sufficient. This shows, he thought, that living in a political community is natural, while living in isolation is not. A second reason is that we have the capacity for speech and the use of moral concepts, and these are the main tools of politics. This means we're built for politics, to live together in political society. And that makes political rule natural.[10]

A common defense of the second premise draws a comparison with the family. We're born into families, and we can't choose our siblings. Yet we still owe them obligations – we owe them care, help, support, maybe even love. Similarly, the naturalist argues, we're born into society. And while we don't get to choose which society we're born into, we still owe it obligations. Central among these is the obligation to obey the law.

There are several problems with this argument. For one, the argument trades on an important ambiguity. The key term here is "member," but that term can mean two different things. On one hand, it can refer to a *descriptive* fact about people. We might say of a person that they are a member of French society, say, because they live there, have a French passport, and so on. On the other hand, the idea of membership can be *moral* or normative. When you join a team, for example, you don't just become a member in the descriptive sense. You also take on certain obligations, show up for practice, pay your membership fees, and help win games. This sense of membership is one that can change the moral landscape.

For the naturalist argument to succeed, the sense of "membership" must be the same, moral one in both (1) and (2) above. Only if we're naturally members of society in the moral sense can we say we're obligated to behave accordingly. If it turns out that we're members in only a descriptive sense, then no such conclusions will follow. After all, any country could issue us a passport. But that wouldn't change our moral landscape.

Aristotle thinks we're morally members of political society because it's natural for us to live that way. But there are two problems here. First, his argument actually doesn't show that we are members. What it shows, if correct, is that it's *better* for us to live as members of political society. It's in our interest to live that way. But even if we can't really live well in isolation, that doesn't make it true that we are members of some society. Many things can be better for us that are not in fact the case. It may be better for you to have eaten more vegetables at lunch. Still, you didn't actually eat them.

Second, ideas about how we must live "naturally" are best approached with caution. History is full of philosophical claims about what's natural that appear silly today. For thousands of years, it was thought natural for men to govern and women to stay at home. It was thought natural that some races are superior to others. It was thought natural that homosexuality was deviant. And on and on. None of these claims are true.

Should we have more faith in Aristotle's claim that membership in political society, in the moral sense, is natural than in those silly claims? It's certainly true, of course, that we can be born members in the descriptive sense. My children were born in the US, and as such are members of American society. They're recognized as citizens, and enjoy the rights that come with that. But we cannot infer from that alone that they also owe moral obligations to the US. The government *says* they are members, and expects their obedience. Our question is whether the government has a right to this. If the answer is yes, there has to be some reason *other* than the government's say-so.

Part of the problem here is that voluntarism isn't so easy to escape, as a philosophical matter. Consider again the comparison with families. True, we don't choose our families, but we're not trapped in them, either. Families can be rejected. And sometimes, that can be a good (if sad) thing. When families don't get along, when they fail to support and care for one another, or when they're even abusive, it can be better for "members" to go their separate ways. In those cases, it seems simply false to say that they're acting wrongly, living unnaturally, or failing to fulfill their obligations. It's important that we have the freedom to leave our families if needed.[11]

Similarly, even if communities – in the moral, meaningful sense – are not chosen, we're not trapped in them, either. This is true for all non-political communities. We are members of many communities, organized around our interests, identity, and friends. Some of these we may grow up with, ones that we never really joined but just belong to. Some will be ones we consciously joined. Either way, we do have the choice to either continue or jettison our membership. And in none of these cases would we accept the idea that we need to emigrate in order to sever these ties.

Aristotle's view that political membership is natural is part of his broader view that there exist natural hierarchies. Naturally, some people are leaders, which means they're supposed to govern, while others are meant to follow. Another example, according to Aristotle, is that some people are naturally meant to be slaves. Aristotle's argument for this is similar to his point about self-sufficiency and government. Just as people "naturally" developed government because they can't live well by themselves, they also "naturally" developed slavery (Aristotle 2014: 1254b). Obviously, this is a terrible argument. Slavery is horrific, and there's no sense in which one can say it's natural that has any moral upshot (other than its being horrific). This argument is bad when applied to slavery, and there's no reason to think it better when applied to politics.

The appeal of voluntarism stems from a morally fundamental principle. Call this the principle of moral equality:

> **Principle of Moral Equality:** People are morally free and equal and, as such, not naturally subordinate to one another.

Voluntarism fully embraces this idea. It accepts that people can *only* be in charge of one another if this is freely chosen. And it accepts this because it sees people as one another's equals. Naturalism denies the principle of moral equality. And while it may seem fine when we're thinking about political society, denying this principle really is a huge deal. The principle forbids men imposing themselves on women, whites imposing themselves on blacks, heterosexuals imposing themselves on LBGTQ+. By extension, it forbids governments imposing themselves on people.

WHAT IF THERE IS NO OBLIGATION TO OBEY?

We are at a crossroads. One road meant giving up on voluntarism, the idea that legitimate political authority must be freely accepted. But doing that threatened the principle of moral equality. There exist, of course, other theories of political obligation, ones we haven't discussed here. Many of these theories claim to reject voluntarism without also rejecting the principle of moral equality. This is a difficult task. It requires showing how minorities who don't want to be part of society can be made subject to the will of the majority without being made subordinate to that majority. People disagree on whether this can be pulled off.

What about the other road? What if, instead of rejecting voluntarism, we give up on the idea that we all have an obligation to obey the law? This option is called *philosophical anarchism*. Philosophical anarchism is not the anarchism you might ordinarily think of. Philosophical anarchists don't go around throwing rocks at cops, think we should burn down the state, and so on. The sense in which they're anarchists is more modest. They're anarchist just in the sense that they believe we don't have a moral obligation to do something just because the law says so.

It's important to get right what this position means. One thing it *doesn't* mean is that you can just break any law you like. Many laws forbid things we already have good moral reason not to do. Theft, violence, trespass, assault, fraud, and endangerment are all things that are simply morally wrong. And they're wrong whether or not they're illegal. In those cases, the philosophical anarchist will agree that we should not do them. They will just insist that the fact that it's prohibited by law doesn't matter morally. We shouldn't do those things simply because they're wrong.[12]

In other cases, the philosophical anarchist position makes a practical difference. If we have political obligations, there will be things we have to do just because our government requires them. Certain tax-and-transfer programs, say, might not be morally obligatory if there is no obligation to obey the law. Think of programs that support the arts. These may well be very worthy, but we might also think that we're not morally *required* to give our money to the arts, except that it's part of a government program. The philosophical anarchist is committed to saying you do no wrong if you shirk supporting such programs (assuming you didn't consent, or otherwise voluntarily accept the obligation to obey the law). You're free, of course, to pay anyway. But it's morally unexceptionable if you don't.

A third kind of case is perhaps most interesting. Supporting the arts is morally fine, but other things our governments do are not. Governments wage wars, run a police force that engages in excessive and racial violence, enact discriminatory laws, and more. The philosophical anarchist will be committed to resist or disobey these things. Since there is no obligation to obey in the first place, the injustice of these laws determines what we should do. By contrast, if we do have political obligations, we may be required to go along with or support laws like this. And even if we are permitted to disobey, we may be required to do it in only certain ways. This topic is often called *civil disobedience*, and we will return to it in Chapter 4.

QUESTIONS

(1) Why can't equals have the right to decide for others how to live?
(2) If governments do not need consent to govern, can we still insist on consent in other parts of life, such as sexual relations? If so, what's the difference?
(3) It's commonly said that minorities need protection from the majority. How small must a minority be before it is no longer entitled to protection? What about a minority of one?

NOTES

1   Rights and obligations are often said to be "correlates." This means that the right of one party (here, the government) can be understood in terms of the obligation of another party (you or me, say). The right of the government to be obeyed can then be explained in terms of the obligation we have to obey, and vice versa. The classical discussion, which also considers other kinds of rights (that correlate to things other than obligations), is Hohfeld (1919).
2   See Chapter 1.
3   The famous phrase "no taxation without representation" captures this idea. It was, of course, adopted by American revolutionaries

as a slogan in their fight against English colonial rule during the American War of Independence. The American Founding Fathers were deeply influenced by Locke's thought.

4 Subsequent citations to this source will contain the Roman numeral of the Treatise and the section number. Here, that would be: II, 199.

5 Note: even if this argument for (5) – the argument Hume is attacking – fails, that does *not* mean that the conclusion in (5) must be false. It may be true for other reasons. So, for all Hume writes, we may all still have political obligations. But it wouldn't be for reasons of consent.

6 Philosophers who write about colonialism and national self-determination often miss this distinction. They think that legitimacy is achieved if the colonized people can have their own elected governments. This argument also confuses the two senses of legitimacy, interpreting the first kind to also cover the second kind.

7 Recall, the Declaration of Independence talks about governments "deriving their just powers from the consent of the governed."

8 When you see people saying this kind of thing, i.e., saying that voting means agreeing but not saying that not-voting means not-agreeing, your philosophical alarm bells should go off. That's often a sign of people making up a nice-sounding story to hold onto their desired conclusions, rather than making an honest argument.

9 The former is often called the "fair-play" theory, defended, for example, by Klosko (2008). The latter is usually attributed to Kant (2017 [1797]). For a recent defense of the latter, see Ripstein (2009).

10 There are more ways Aristotle thought political society was natural, such as that it arose out of more "primitive" natural associations like villages and households.

11 You, like me, may know people whose families have rejected them for their sexuality. For people in this situation, it's important to have the ability to cut ties. Even if, in the end, they choose not to leave.

12 Of course, something being illegal may matter in other non-moral ways. You may want to avoid breaking the law because you are likely to be caught and punished . But that's a different type of concern.

FREEDOM AND EQUALITY

Theories of political obligation and authority face a difficult task. They have to find a balance between two competing ideas. As the Genevan philosopher Jean-Jacques Rousseau (1712–1778) put it in the opening sentences of *The Social Contract*: "Man is born free; and everywhere he is in chains … How did this change come about? I do not know. What can make it legitimate? That question I think I can answer" (Rousseau 1923 [1762]: bk. 1, ch. 1).

People are *free and equal*, Rousseau thought, meaning they are born in charge of their own lives, subordinate to none. There are no natural bosses. Governments, however, claim to be in charge of us. The kind of authority they claim cannot be possessed by any ordinary person.

Different theories try to balance these ideas in different ways. Naturalism, the theory that politics is natural and authority doesn't have to be freely accepted, prizes the importance of government and social order. But its insistence on natural hierarchies between people raises the worry that it effectively negates our freedom and equality. Consent theory, by contrast, holds firm on freedom and equality, but calls into serious question the legitimacy of government. Other theories offer different trade-offs, falling on different places on this spectrum.

DOI: 10.4324/9781003250692-4

To better understand these trade-offs, we need to know more about freedom and equality. Why should we think of people as free and equal? Are these values really at odds with political authority? What do freedom and equality even mean? And who counts as such?

EARLY ATTACKS ON INEQUALITY

For most philosophers today, people being free and equal is a starting point for their theories. In whatever ways a theory might be attractive, it can't deny that we all have this status. Or at least it can't deny this without facing a significant uphill battle. The idea may be almost a fixed point in our thinking. Other claims, arguments, and principles have to fit around it.

Things used to be different. The claim that all people are free and equal has only relatively recently become widely accepted. For a very long time, this was considered a radical, even dangerous thought. To say people are free and equal was to fray the fabric of society, challenging the hierarchies that held together large groups of people in peace and harmony. Kings, emperors, and other leaders had long based their rule on such claims.

In this context, it was radical to ask for a reason why rulers should be in charge, what gave them the right to rule over others. To raise that question was to challenge the very foundations of social and political order. Few did more to raise it than the English philosopher Thomas Hobbes (1588–1679). Hobbes is often associated with his defense of powerful, authoritarian governments. But while Hobbes did believe such governments were desirable, this conclusion is far from the most interesting thing about his thought. More interesting are his arguments, which include an attack on the claim that people are naturally unequal.

Hobbes used a famous thought experiment, the *state of nature*, to question this claim. A state of nature is an imaginary condition in which no government exists. It's what would happen if people lived together without a state or centralized source of public authority. We can use this thought experiment to better understand the role we want government to play, and how it might come about in a way that's morally or rationally acceptable.[1]

In a state of nature, Hobbes thought, we're all on our own. There are no police to call for protection. And this means people are equal: "Nature hath made men so equall … the weakest has strength enough to kill the strongest, either by secret machination, or by confederacy with others, that are in the same danger with himselfe" (Hobbes 1997 [1651]: ch. XIII). No one is so strong or smart that they can dominate and oppress everyone else. When it comes to protecting ourselves, we're all in the same boat – we're all equal.

Equality has major political implications, according to Hobbes. A state of nature, filled with equal people, will be a very violent place.[2] And that means each of us has very good reason to want a government. Because only a government can protect us. More precisely, each of us *equally* has reason to want a government: we all equally need protection. This means that no one is entitled to special treatment from government. We all make the same deal when we accept life under a government. After all, we need protection from others, but they need protection from us just as much. And since we're all making such a deal, we all must be better off living under government. Political rule has to be good for everyone, not just some privileged group or majority. The very legitimacy of government depends on it.

This argument directly contradicts ideas of natural hierarchy or some having a special right to rule. Hobbes replaced such ideas with a functionalist theory of government. Functionalist theories hold that, since no one is personally morally entitled to rule, governments must earn their authority. And they earn it by performing a certain function. For Hobbes, this function is protecting us from the dangers of a state of nature. If the government keeps you safe, it gets to be the boss. If it fails to keep you safe, it loses all authority.

Hobbes was attracted to this theory because he lived through the English Civil War (1642–1651). The Civil War was a long and bloody conflict in which the English Crown and Parliament fought one another over the right to rule. Authority and order broke down, and England devolved into something like a state of nature. People who used to be friends and neighbors became enemies, killing one another and destroying one another's homes and livelihoods. Hobbes saw firsthand just how awful things can get when there is no government to keep the peace.

The war started because the king and Parliament both claimed they, and not the other, really had the right to rule.[3] In a situation like that, Hobbes argued, claims about natural rights to rule are of no use. When Parliament denied the king's birthright to govern, insisting that he really had such a right simply wasn't convincing anyone. And so, the fighting continued. The solution, Hobbes argued, is to accept that ideas like birth or tradition have nothing to do with authority. What matters is who best provides security. If that were Parliament, then it would be the legitimate authority. If it were the king, we ought to obey him.

Equality, for Hobbes, is a *political* idea. It speaks to what we want from government. Equality describes our relative standing with respect to the state – it says that we're all equally positioned with respect to government and the rules it enforces. If superheroes lived among us, things might be different. Superheroes don't need the same protections as the rest of us, so perhaps they could have some claim to special treatment. But for regular people who all need a government in order to be safe, equality is the norm. Legitimate political institutions must treat us equally.

EQUALITY AS A MORAL IDEA

Hobbes dismissed ideas like natural or moral rights, especially the right to be an authority. His worry was that such ideas can be destabilizing. They are often used to challenge and dislodge effective authority, and Hobbes thought that was very dangerous.

Others are less skeptical. John Locke thought government legitimacy doesn't only depend on the authorities doing their job, but also on doing it in a morally acceptable way. Governments have their powers over us in trust, and to keep that trust, they must protect and respect our rights. This is why they cannot rule without first receiving the consent of the people.

Consent matters because people have rights that prevent them from being subjected to authority against their will. But that means our rights must be moral or natural, not (merely) legal or political. These latter sorts of rights are defined by governments themselves, after all. And that makes it trivially easy for them to respect those rights.

Our natural rights shield us from unconsented-to authority, for Locke, because those rights protect our freedom and equality. They safeguard our moral standing, the fact that we're born beholden to no one. Locke understood freedom as people's ability to "to order their Actions, within the bounds of the Law of Nature, without asking leave, or depending upon the Will of any other Man" (Locke 1988 [1689]: II, 4). To be free, in other words, is to be in charge of how you live. Locke understood equality to mean that "all the Power and Jurisdiction is reciprocal, no one having more than another" (Locke 1988 [1689]: II, 4). Whatever rights you have, everyone else must have as well.

Freedom and equality are defined quite differently here than in Hobbes' thought. Whereas Hobbes thinks we are equal because free people are equally threatening to one another, Locke thinks of freedom and equality in *juridical* terms. These terms refer to the *rights* we have over ourselves and one another. We're free because we're entitled to decide how we live (as long as we don't violate other people's rights). We're equal because initially everyone has exactly the same rights as others.

Locke offers a brief argument for why we're equal in this way: "Creatures of the same species and rank promiscuously born to all the same advantages of Nature, and the use of the same faculties, should also be equal one amongst another without Subordination or Subjection" (Locke 1988 [1689]: II, 4).

We're equal because we're all, in some relevant way, the same. Nature gave us the same "advantages" and "faculties" and this similarity makes us equal. The argument appeals to the idea that it's rational to treat like cases alike. If two things are the same, in relevant respects, then we can't reasonably treat them as if they are different. Since people are the same in all *morally* relevant respects, they ought to be treated equally.

To be legitimate, governments must respect us as free and equal beings in this moralized sense. This significantly restricts the kind of politics in which they can engage. Whatever authority a government possesses will be whatever the people have willingly bestowed on it (all other power being blocked by our natural rights). And such authority is always held in trust, ready to be revoked in case of abuse of power. To claim more power than this would be to claim power over people without their consent. That's to claim to have rights over them that they do not have over others. Among equals, that cannot be.

As with Hobbes, the implication is that no one is entitled to special privilege or treatment. As equals, we all make the same deal with the government when we consent to its rule, and we expect equal treatment in return. But, in contrast to Hobbes, more is at stake when governments overstep the boundaries of their authority. Whereas for Hobbes, such transgressions threaten the legitimacy of government, for Locke, abuse of power also constitutes a specific kind of wrong. It's a wrong done to the people, in violation of their rights.

Locke used this idea to great effect. He argued that absolute governments (the kind of governments with unlimited power, like the one Hobbes accepted) could never be legitimate. Since governments have to respect our rights, and their job is to make us safer, it would never make sense for the people to give them absolute power. Such power effectively erases our rights, destroying our standing as free and equal. Only a fool would give a government absolute authority. Since people aren't fools, absolute authority can never be legitimate. That kind of inequality is impossible (Locke 1988 [1689]: II, 137).

CHANGING IDEAS OF FREEDOM AND EQUALITY

The equality we find in Hobbes and Locke is like equality before the law. To be treated as equals is to be subject to the same rules, applied impartially. Arbitrary power violates this equality because it claims either rights that no one can possess, or rights that people would never give away. This means the rules of morality are applied unevenly, or not even applied at all. Let's call this equality – in which all are subject to the same rules, applied impartially – *process-equality*.

Process-equality allows for people's lives to go quite differently. You might be rich, I might be poor, but as long as this happened under a uniform set of rules, impartially applied, our equal moral status is not offended. The result is that we might see quite a lot of inequality in other terms, including material inequality. The idea of process-equality simply doesn't speak to that. Lady Justice wears a blindfold – she doesn't take sides between rich and poor. As long as the processes were fair, and fairly applied, from this point of view, no problematic inequalities exist.

As societies became wealthier, this idea of equality became increasingly worrisome to people. Some were riding around in carriages, wearing fancy clothes, and eating fine foods, while others worked in dire conditions, for little pay, barely even getting enough calories to be healthy. Even if the processes leading up to this were fair (although usually they weren't), such outcomes still strike many as unfair. When our lives go that differently, the thought goes, we're really not treated as if we matter to the same degree. Such outcomes seem to violate a different idea of equality. Call this idea *outcome-equality*.[4]

Just as there's a difference in focus between process-equality and outcome-equality, a related difference can be detected in notions of freedom. Early modern thinkers saw freedom as something that's threatened mainly by interference from others.[5] But the worry that underpins about outcome-equality casts doubt on that. Rich people seemed significantly freer than poor people. But poverty doesn't limit your freedom because you're facing a lot more interference. When you're poor, you have fewer options and opportunities than when you're rich. And that seems to mean you enjoy less freedom.

You can be less free, in other words, when you aren't able to *do* certain things, to live your life certain ways. And this is true even if no one is interfering with you. The type of freedom is often called *positive* freedom, a term coined by the British philosopher Isaiah Berlin (1909–1997). The contrasting idea of freedom, freedom as the absence of interference, Berlin called *negative* freedom (Berlin 1969).

Lots of philosophical questions surround these ideas. For instance, the two conceptions of equality seem at times to conflict. Process-equality is about everyone being subject to the same rules, but people living and working under those rules can end up with very different material holdings. Outcome-equality wants to correct this, but that means upending processes that (otherwise) looked perfectly fair. Making outcomes more equal means taxing some more than others, restricting who may be hired or admitted to educational institutions, offering special assistance programs to specific groups of people, and so on. Such measures seem to violate process-equality. We must choose which kind of equality we really care about.[6]

Defenders of outcome-equality sometimes argue that there is no conflict between process-equality and their aims. We're all subject to the same rules, it's said, even when some people enjoy burdens or benefits that others do not. The rich pay more taxes, but we all live under one set of rules. It's just that those rules say that *if* you are rich, then you must pay more.

That's perfectly fair and equal treatment. Others are less convinced. When you're paying multiples of what your neighbor pays in taxes, the fact that things could have been different had you not been financially successful might provide little solace. You may still feel you're bearing burdens that others avoid.

It's relatively easy to see the value and appeal of process-equality. When people are treated unevenly by authorities, that's a paradigmatic violation of their moral equality. Such treatment conflicts with the relation we each have with government. Many people find the goal of some forms of outcome-equality intuitively obvious, too. But the value and appeal of this sense of equality are more difficult to explain. Some people think things being equal just seems fairer, and that's all there is to it. But we all live different lives, work different jobs, spend our money differently, and choose to take more or fewer financial risks. In that context, a context in which at least some unequal outcomes are the result of people's choices, the argument that more equal means fairer becomes harder to maintain.[7]

Sometimes it's suggested that unequal outcomes are a sign of unequal processes – that the differences we see in society are evidence that some people are more privileged, receiving various unfair advantages. The existence of significant differences in living standards might be evidence that the law is applied unevenly. Measures to achieve more outcome-equality can then be presented as measures to correct for this unfairness in terms of process-equality. This is fair enough. Often there exist unequal advantages, and often these are the result of unfair treatment by governments. But as an argument, this doesn't establish what we set out to show: the value of outcome-equality as an ideal. This argument explains the value of outcome-equality in terms of process-equality. We should care about more equal outcomes because those would be the outcomes we'd see if the processes in society were indeed equal. But that raises the same question: what if the processes are fair, but we still see unequal outcomes?

Perhaps it's tempting to say that fair processes just are those processes that lead to equal outcomes. But this won't do. We're looking for a reason why we should care about equal outcomes in the first place, and this argument leads us to think in a circle. If we say:

(1)   Fair processes matter because they lead to equal outcomes,

but we also say that:

(2)   Equal outcomes matter because they result from fair processes,

then we're explaining (1) in terms of (2) and (2) in terms of (1). We're saying that equal processes matter because they lead to equal outcomes, and that equal outcomes matter because they're the result of equal processes. That can't be.

It's possible, of course, to appeal to yet other reasons to pursue outcome-equality. One popular argument holds that other important rights become endangered if significant material inequality exists. Another sees inequality as dangerous because it means we don't all have an equal say in politics anymore, and this threatens democracy. Such arguments may or may not be true, but they understand the value of outcome-equality in terms of other goals. We still lack a reason to care about outcome-equality as such.

FREEDOM, EQUALITY, AND SUBJECTION

There's a connection between our ideas of freedom and equality, on the one hand, and the role we see for government, on the other. For instance, achieving outcome-equality typically requires government action. To reduce income inequality, say, we need a system of taxation, economic regulation, and redistribution. This requires society to be regulated by political and legal institutions. Accordingly, outcome-equality is often seen as something that can be achieved only via the state.

Some theories even see equality as something that can be *uniquely* achieved under government. On this view, there is a difference between being subjected to a person and being subjected to political authority. Equality means there exist no natural hierarchies between people. When we're subject to a person, we're being treated as less than equal, because it involves them imposing their will on us. But the state is impersonal, this argument goes. It's a public entity charged with upholding justice and equality between people, standing above us in a way that no private person ever could. Its decisions imply no greater or lesser standing.[8]

This approach is starkly different from the early understandings of freedom and equality we began with. Those effectively worked to challenge and limit political authority. Locke and Hobbes used equality to argue that governments cannot have any special claims of authority. They must earn their authority in the same way you or I would have to, through consent (for Locke) or performance (for Hobbes). Governments are made of people, and so the same standards of equality apply to them as to us.

By contrast, this alternative approach sees equality as perfectly consistent with political authority. This idea is most plausible in a democracy. Democracies give every person a vote equal to that of everyone else's. And so our power over one another remains equal, in the sense that there's no one whose decisions we're subjected to who's not likewise subjected to our decisions as well.

The most famous version of this argument is Rousseau's *The Social Contract*. According to Rousseau, a democracy is ruled by the "General Will." This is a form of all of our wills put together, purified through democratic deliberation. The General Will respects our equality because it includes all of our ideas, arguments, and decisions. No other form of legislation can say the same. Rousseau thought that the General Will also ensures that we remain perfectly free. Since we're subject only to laws that we helped create ourselves, we're never bound by laws that we didn't give to ourselves. All laws reflect our own wills and, as a result, we remain entirely free when we live in a democracy (Rousseau 1923 [1762]: bk. 2, ch. 3).

In fact, in one of his more famous and paradoxical remarks, Rousseau wrote that we can force people to live in a democracy without violating their freedom or equality. To be forced to live this way, he wrote, just is to be "forced to be free" (Rousseau 1923 [1762]: bk. 1, ch. 7). The argument goes roughly as follows:

(1) If you're forced to live in a democracy, you're forced to obey the General Will.
(2) The General Will unites our individual wills.
(3) Therefore, if you're forced to live in a democracy, you're forced to obey a will that includes your own.
(4) Nobody who is forced to obey a will that includes their own will is being treated as unfree or less than equal.
(5) Therefore, nobody who's forced to live in a democracy is being treated as unfree or less than equal.

This argument promises to unify freedom and equality with forced subjection to government. But there are some reasons to worry. For one, the argument depends on the truth of premise (2), claiming that the General Will (i.e., democratic legislation) unites our individual wills. This seems most plausible if democratic deliberation requires unanimous agreement. If we all literally agreed to the law, we can have no objection to it. But, of course, such unanimity is very difficult to find. And no democracy exists that uses it as a decision-rule.

Most followers of Rousseau think that we can preserve the truth of premise (2) without unanimity. The idea is that, while democratic legislation may not unite our actual wills, it can still reflect the kinds of reasons that matter to us all. In order to sway the legislature, the arguments we use in democratic decision-making have to appeal to such reasons. Self-interested, ideological, or irrational reasons will not suffice to convince others.

What's needed are rational and impartial reasons, ones that are acceptable to others as well as to us. Legislative decisions, then, reflect reasons that are rationally and impartially defensible. And such reasons do not conflict with our wills, or at least not the parts of our wills that we ought to care about.

This, roughly, is known as the theory of "public reason." The most detailed and influential version of it is offered by the American philosopher John Rawls (1921–2002) in his book *Political Liberalism* (Rawls 2005 [1993]). The theory holds that democratically acceptable laws are laws that reasonable people can't reject. If successful, this could serve Rousseau's purposes. Being forced to do what's reasonable is to follow what the reasonable parts of our wills dictate anyway. This is no violation of our freedom and equality. And properly functioning democracies pass only such reasonable laws.

We can now replace the previous argument with the following similar, but slightly different one:

(1')   If you're forced to live in a democracy, you're forced to obey only democratically acceptable laws.

(2')   Democratically acceptable laws are based on rational and impartial reasons.

(3')   Therefore, if you're forced to live in a democracy, you're forced to obey only laws that are based on rational and impartial reasons.

(4')   Nobody who obeys only rational and impartial reasons is being treated as unfree or less than equal.

(5')   Therefore, nobody who's forced to live in a democracy is being treated as unfree or less than equal.

Rousseau's conclusion can remain, then. Even when we don't like the laws our democratic legislature passes, we're not wronged when we're forced to obey.

This is a tricky position to defend. Premise (2) is false under majority rule systems, where one can find oneself outvoted by the majority. Whether (2') is true will depend on the peculiarities of democratic deliberation. And, to many, it will seem like a stretch to say that legislatures like the US Congress pass only laws that are reasonable and impartial.

But even if (2') is true, the bigger problem is the shift from (4) to (4') that it requires. According to (4'), whether our freedom and equality are violated depends on whether we're forced to do things we *should* want, things we'd want if we were rational and impartial reasoners. This is a peculiar idea. It suggests that our freedom and equality depend on the kind of reasons we have for doing things. But that conflicts with paradigmatic examples of denials of freedom or equality. Suppose you think I'm overweight and force me to diet. Say, you threaten to hurt me any time I reach for a snack. Surely, whether you thereby limit my freedom does not depend on whether I have good reason to diet. I'm either free to eat what I want or not, and whether or not I should lose weight is irrelevant to that. The argument above implies otherwise.

Are people who reason badly protected by rights? If the protections of our freedom and equality depend on whether we reason correctly, in a manner fit for the General Will, then the answer must be no. After all, people who reason poorly can be forced to comply with the General Will, even if it goes against their actual (defective) will. But being so forced seems a paradigmatic rights-violation. The protections of our rights ought to protect the irrational and impetuous just as much as they do the rational and collected. Again, Rousseau's view implies otherwise.

WHO COUNTS AS FREE AND EQUAL?

In Locke's description, freedom and equality are the "State all Men are naturally in." For Locke, "all Men" meant "all human beings," but this was certainly not the common view in his time. It had long been accepted that while *some* people were free and equal, this was certainly not true of everyone. Equality means treating people the same when they're alike in morally relevant respects. But women, Jews, foreigners, racial minorities, and other minority groups were seen as different, and therefore inferior.

An important early critic of the exclusion of women was the English philosopher Mary Wollstonecraft (1759–1797). In *A Vindication of the Rights of Woman*, Wollstonecraft provided a forceful defense of women's status as free and equal to men (Wollstonecraft 2009 [1792]). Like Locke and Rousseau and many others, Wollstonecraft thought that such status depends on our capacity for reason. The thesis of her *Vindication* is that women have the same capacity to reason as men and are therefore to be included in the class of free and equal beings.

Wollstonecraft wanted to show that the community of equals was larger than many thought. To do this, she had to demonstrate that the community of reasonable creatures included women. Patriarchal theories denied this by claiming that women were more emotional than men, less stable, more beholden to vices like jealousy, excessive materialism, gossiping, and so on. Interestingly, Wollstonecraft agreed with these charges. She conceded that the women of her time often behaved less rationally than men. But crucially, she argued, this didn't show they had any less *capacity* for reason. The patriarchal mistake was to think feminine irrational traits were natural facts, something inherently female.

Wollstonecraft argued that these traits instead were the result of social facts. They are what happens when society denies people who have the capacity for reason the opportunity to develop it. Rational beings whose development is stunted by social and political oppression will develop deformities and so, instead of becoming virtuous, rational, and strong, women became vicious, emotional, and soft. This certainly called for a response, Wollstonecraft thought. But the remedy was not to deny women their rights. It was to offer them the same education, freedom, and opportunities to work that men enjoy.

The inclusion of women and others as free and equal beings further challenged traditional notions of social and political order.

Just as kings or noble families were said to be entitled to rule the land, men were said to be the heads of household, with women subservient. When such presumed hierarchies are replaced by the ideal of equality, new questions arise. What ties us together as human beings? How can free and equal people live together? Do we owe the same to every person in the world, or should we prioritize our families, friends, or even our fellow citizens?

These questions arise because at every step of growing the community of free and equal beings, we may wonder whether we've reached its true borders. Even if historically, many people have been wrongly excluded, and those borders were drawn too narrowly, the community of equals does need boundaries. Cows don't have the same rights as you or me – they are not free and equal beings. That's not to say that we can treat them any way we like (you should stop eating them), but it would be silly to say they have a right to vote.

To identify certain beings as free and equal is to answer a political question. It says who counts the same in terms of their rights, freedoms, claims, and interests. The Locke-Rousseau-Wollstonecraft view holds that capacity for reason makes us free and equal, because it sets up the main challenge of politics. Given that it's not appropriate to boss around beings who can make their own decisions (or at least not without good justification), how can we justify governmental authority?[9]

The ideas of freedom and equality typically come up as part of critiques of social or political relations or institutions. They identify problematic ways in which government or society treats people. Such complaints identify unacceptable relations of servitude or dependence, forms of treatment that are objectionable, or unfair differences in how our lives go. To understand what freedom and equality mean today, we need to ask what social and political problems currently exist. What are the most glaring forms of subservience and dependence that threaten our ability to live by our own lights, subservient to no one? Answering that helps us better see the full meaning of freedom and equality.

We might not reach a full or complete understanding of these concepts. Once we achieve one kind of equality, we often see new and important ways in which we're failing to meet these ideals. Many early arguments against inequality might not look very egalitarian today. The power of aristocracy was challenged by the claim that all male citizens who owned property should count as equals. This undercut feudal power and widened the circle of people who counted as equals. But that circle remained very narrow. Still, once accepted, such limited arguments often take on a life of their own. Small increases in who counts as free and equal start growing, further expanding the community of equals. Steadily, such arguments have grown into the radical ideas we accept as true today: that we're *all* free and equal.

QUESTIONS

(1) No government allows you to refuse to pay taxes. Does that make you less free?

(2) Is an equalized society the same thing as a society of equals?

(3) If aliens landed on Earth tomorrow, would they count as free and equal to us?

NOTES

1 Thought experiments, like other experiments, aim to isolate a certain variable in order to study how it behaves. In philosophy, thought experiments isolate a particular idea. We imagine a situation in which all other ideas or variables are held constant, or are assumed not to exist, and ask how the idea we're investigating behaves in that context. (This is why it's not uncommon for philosophical thought experiments to get a little weird. But sometimes that's the best, or only, way to isolate a certain idea.)

2 Hobbes' argument for this claim is discussed in Chapter 4.

3 More precisely, at issue were the right to decide things like religious practices, such as whether or not to use the Book of Common Prayer, as well as taxation.

4 There exists an intricate philosophical literature about precisely what outcomes are to be equalized, in order for outcome-equality to be achieved. Some argue equality concerns resources, others opportunities, yet others our ability to function in certain ways. For these arguments, see Dworkin (1981a; 1981b); Cohen (1989); Sen (1999) respectively.

5 This simplifies, of course. For instance, Hobbes understood liberty as "the absence of externall Impediments" (Hobbes 1997 [1651]: ch. XIV). Locke insisted that we're not free to do things that are wrong, since "*a State of Liberty ... is not a State of Licence*" (Locke 1988 [1689]: II, 6). Nevertheless, from a political point of view, both saw other people (wrongfully) interfering with our choices as the main threat to freedom.

6 This issue can be seen in the US Supreme Court decision *Students for Fair Admissions v. Harvard*, 600 U.S. 181 (2023). Supporters of affirmative action admission propose policies of selective admissions to universities in an effort to achieve greater outcome-equality. But opponents insist that these measures violate process-equality, by disadvantaging innocent students. The US political and legal system seems to want to care about both kinds of equality, but had to make a decision here. In the end, the Court prioritized process-equality and sided with the opponents of affirmative action.

7 One theory about outcome-equality holds that outcomes should be equal except when inequalities are the result of people's choices. This view is called *luck-egalitarianism* (because it holds that there ought to be no inequalities that are the result of mere luck). See e.g. Cohen (1989). For an influential critique, see Anderson (1999).

8 The most pronounced version of this argument comes from Immanuel Kant. In the *Doctrine of Right*, Kant called the law an "omnilateral will," something he distinguished from the will of another person, which he called a "bilateral will." According to Kant, our equality prohibits us from being subjected to bilateral wills, but not from being subjected to the omnilateral will (Kant 2017 [1797]). The best recent treatment is Ripstein (2009).

9 Note the difference from Hobbes, for whom the main problem of politics was not justifying authority but avoiding civil war.

THE SOCIAL CONTRACT

The central question of Rousseau's *The Social Contract* is how free and equal beings can be bound by the rules of their societies. The voluntarist answers that governments have authority if their people voluntarily choose to give them authority. But of course, that rarely happens. Most of us never made such a choice. And some might not even agree to if they were asked. Rousseau proposed an alternative. If people *would have* chosen to obey the laws, had they thought about it carefully, that's good enough. They'd be morally bound to follow the rules of society.

This is the idea behind the social contract. The social contract is not a real contract – it's not some piece of paper we actually sign. It's an imaginary or postulated agreement between the people who live together in society. That imagined agreement defines the acceptable rules of living together, including what's right and wrong, who gets to be in charge, and what we must do to help one another. If we can suppose that we all would be willing to enter into such an agreement, then we can suppose that its terms will be acceptable to everyone. While that's not quite the same thing as people actually agreeing to obey the rules, it might be enough to say that no one is wrongfully forced to obey the law.

DOI: 10.4324/9781003250692-5

Imagined agreements are different from actual agreements, of course. The most important and obvious difference is that they didn't actually happen. And, usually, agreements have to happen before they matter. You have to actually sign your lease before you can live in a house. Still, social contract theorists think that for things like social rules, imaginary or hypothetical agreement can be meaningful. This chapter discusses the idea of a social contract and what, if anything, this idea of hypothetical agreement might mean for politics. We'll look at how it affects our moral obligation to obey the law as well as justice more generally.

HOBBES ON THE STATE OF NATURE

Before Rousseau, Hobbes proposed a theory of the social contract. In *Leviathan*, Hobbes argued that a social contract is the solution to the problems of the state of nature, the condition without the existence of government. These problems, Hobbes famously wrote, are that life in a state of nature will be "solitary, poore, nasty, brutish, and short" (Hobbes 1997 [1651]: ch. XIII). And in order to escape them, rational people would join together in political society, choosing to live together under a single sovereign with the power to keep them safe. That agreement could actually happen. But even if it didn't, and a powerful sovereign imposed itself and kept them safe, the underlying deal would remain the same. We are bound to obey when government keeps us safe.

This idea was radically different from other political theories in Hobbes' time. Drawing inspiration from the work of the Italian philosopher Thomas Aquinas (1225–1274), it was common to argue that the key to a good and safe society is good and peaceful citizens. When society turns to violence and civil war, its people are acting aggressively and wickedly, and the only way to solve that is to make them be better. The main job of a good government, therefore, was said to make people become more virtuous and upstanding citizens.

Hobbes understood that this could not be correct. Having seen the English Civil War up close, he'd witnessed how the very same people who were once peaceful neighbors came to be at each other's throats. It made no sense to say that these people, who had been good citizens just recently, had suddenly become bad or wicked people. Something else was going on.

Hobbes' assessment of what was happening is among the most celebrated arguments in the history of political philosophy. According to Hobbes, it's not the people as such that are the problem. It's the circumstances they live in. People want peace, wherever they live. But sometimes circumstances cooperate, sometimes they don't. And there can be circumstances in which people who really want peace may feel forced to act violently and aggressively. Societies that want to avoid war, therefore, need to avoid these kinds of circumstances.

This idea of is often overlooked. Many people think that Hobbes says that people are naturally violent. But it's easy to see that that cannot be his point. The state of nature sets us up to be at war, according to Hobbes. The argument goes as follows:

(1)   The state of nature lacks effective government.
(2)   If there's no effective government, the only way to be safe is to protect yourself.
(3)   Therefore, in a state of nature, the only way to be safe is to protect yourself.
(4)   The best way to protect yourself is to attack others before they threaten you.
(5)   Therefore, in a state of nature, the best way to be safe is to attack others before they threaten you.

Premise (1) is true by definition. Premise (2) simply states what it's like when there are no police to call. This much seems straightforward. Since (3) follows directly from (1) and (2), the crux of the argument is premise (4). This is the idea that, when we have to protect ourselves, the best defense is offense. To be safe, we need to fight in preemptive self-defense. And that's why people will end up fighting.

The argument for this claim comes in two steps. The first identifies what Hobbes called the "Laws of Nature." These are "precepts" of reason, meaning principles that every rational person must follow. The fundamental idea behind these laws is the need for self-preservation. The first order of business in life is staying alive, and so the most fundamental task for any rational person is to avoid death. Several things follow for how we should live. Most important among these is what Hobbes terms the first and "Fundamental" Law of Nature:

> it is a precept, or generall rule of Reason, *That every man, ought to endeavour Peace, as farre as he has hope of obtaining it; and when he cannot obtain it, that he may seek, and use, all helps, and advantages of Warre.*
>
> (Hobbes 1997 [1651]: ch. XIV)

Because the best way to stay alive is usually to avoid getting into any fights, rational people are peaceful. The First Law of Nature thus tells us that we should avoid violence as much as possible. At the same time, we cannot afford to avoid violence at all costs. No one is required to let others hurt or kill them. That would be irrational, given that life's first order of business is staying alive. When others threaten us, we get to defend ourselves.

Note that the First Law of Nature is sensitive to circumstance. Whether it's rational for us to seek or avoid violence will depend on our surroundings. When we're safe, it's wrong to initiate conflict. But when we're in danger, we're always allowed to defend ourselves.

The second step of Hobbes' argument holds that the state of nature is always dangerous, and here Hobbes' insight appears. Imagine living in a place without government. It's just you and a bunch of strangers out there, and you know that you're all desperately trying to stay alive. Suppose now that you come across one of these strangers somewhere. What should you do?

The First Law of Nature tells you to stay alive. This means being peaceful when you can, but fighting if you have to. It might seem that each of you should just leave the other alone. Or maybe you should even help each other against aggressors. But while this sounds like a good plan, Hobbes argued that it is not possible. The problem is that you can't be sure whether you can trust the stranger. There's no government to protect you in case they're trouble, after all. That means you're in a very dangerous situation. If you trust the stranger not to attack, and you turn out to be wrong, you might end up seriously hurt or dead. The First Law of Nature tells us it's irrational to trust strangers in this situation. You should attack the other person preemptively, defend yourself before they have a chance to attack you first. That's what self-preservation, and thus reason, require.

Hobbes calls this *anticipation*:

> [T]here is no way for any man to secure himselfe, so rea-sonable, as Anticipation; that is, by force, or wiles, to master the persons of all men he can, so long, till he see no other power great enough to endanger him: And this is no more than his own conservation requireth, and is generally allowed.

(Hobbes 1997 [1651]: ch. XIII)

But now we can see the problem – the other person is in exactly the same situation. They, too, have to take care of their own safety. And they, too, cannot know whether you're to be trusted. Worse, they can be pretty sure you are not to be trusted. After all, they know what you know: reason requires peace when one can afford it, aggression when one can't. Since you can't trust them, *you* may well attack preemptively. And that means this stranger should definitely attack you pre-emptively. Worse yet, you know this about them, making it doubly certain that you should attack preemptively. And they know you know. And you know they know you know. And so on.

The result is a war of all against all. As Hobbes put it:

> Hereby it is manifest, that during the time men live without a common Power to keep them all in awe, they are in that condition which is called Warre; and such a warre, as is of every man, against every man.
>
> (Hobbes 1997 [1651]: ch. XIII)

Again, this is a point about circumstance. This war of all against all happens *not* because we're bad people. Paradoxically, it happens precisely because people want to stay safe. They just happen to be caught in a situation where they can't secure peace without taking unacceptable risks. When we're living in a condition where we have to look out for our own self-preservation, no one can afford to play nice. We can predict what others will do, and reason tells us to attack, in anticipation, before being attacked.

The result is what's often called a *Prisoners' Dilemma*. And Prisoners' Dilemmas are tragic. In this situation, peace and cooperation would clearly be best for everyone. Yet still we all end up fighting. The problem is that what's good for everyone *together* is not the same as what's good for everyone *individually*. And we have to act as individuals. But individually rational actions can lead to collectively irrational outcomes. Peace-seeking individuals end up in civil war.[1]

We've been looking at a situation in which our two options were to fight or not, but the same type of problem occurs in many other contexts. Consider, for example, contracts. Suppose you run a company and want to buy a shipment of machine parts from me. We draw up a contract in which I promise to deliver the goods and you promise to pay me money. In a state of nature, who performs first? Would you send me your money before I send you the parts? How can you trust me to do my part? After all, you can't call the police if I don't. And I certainly won't be sending you the parts first. Because I know that once you have the parts, you may see no reason to pay me anymore.

Here's how Hobbes put it:

> If a Covenant be made, wherein neither of the parties per-forme presently, but trust one another; in the condition of meer Nature, (which is a condition of Warre of every man against every man,) upon any reasonable suspition, it is Voyd; … For he that performeth first, has no assurance the other will performe after; because the bonds of words are too weak to bridle mens ambition, avarice, anger, and other Passions, without the feare of some coerceive Power; which in the condition of meer Nature, where all men are equall, and judges of the justnesse of their own fears cannot possi-bly be supposed. And therefore he which performeth first, does but betray himselfe to his enemy; contrary to the Right (he can never abandon) of defending his life, and means of living.
>
> (Hobbes 1997 [1651]: ch. XIV)

The result, of course, is that the sale never gets done. But now we're both much worse off. I would have liked to have the money more than I wanted to keep the parts. You wanted the parts more than the money. Neither of us got what we wanted. Again, the problem is anticipation. We're smart enough to think ahead, and we can see that without a government, we can't trust one another. The result is that everyone suffers.

THE SOCIAL CONTRACT AND AGREEMENT

The solution to these problems is to change the situation in which people interact. Rather than everyone having to pro-tect themselves, we need some external force capable of mak-ing sure no one attacks, cheats, or otherwise does wrong.

When we're protected by such enforcement, our dealings are safe. If you pay me for those machine parts, and I don't deliver, you can call the cops. And since I can anticipate this possibility, you probably won't have to call the cops. You can just trust me to deliver.

Enforcement ends the problems of the state of nature, then. The force required to constrain behavior comes from government, the state apparatus with the power to issue and enforce laws, keep us safe, and uphold contracts. Government is created by everyone in society coming together and agreeing to form a single society, ruled by a single power. We agree to have a single authority tell us what to do, and to do as we're told by it. We agree to help the government enforce its rules, whether that's by simply obeying the law ourselves, by serving in the military, or by joining the police. Whatever keeps society safe, we agree to do it.

This agreement to create and follow government power is the social contract. Our agreement need not be explicit. And it doesn't even have to be voluntary (Hobbes 1997 [1651]: ch. XIV). All that's needed, according to Hobbes, is that we have good *reason* to agree. This is different from normal contracts. Normally, having reason to agree isn't the same as actually agreeing. In order to agree, we have to do explicitly accept a proposal, sign a contract, or something similar. And we have to do so freely. To say we accepted something just because we had reason to accept is simply mistaken. No one is bound without their actual consent.

But the social contract is different, Hobbes thinks. We form the social contract in the state of nature, and ideas like "right and wrong" or "just and unjust" simply have no place there. These are creations of government. Since there is no government yet in the state of nature, we can have no complaint when authority and enforcement are imposed on us (Hobbes 1997 [1651]: ch. XIII). It can be in our interest, or not in our interest, to go along with such enforced rules. But it cannot be right or wrong. And, of course, Hobbes thinks it's very much in our interest to go along with them. Our reason to accept the social contract is our very safety and survival.

Hobbes' claim that ideas like right and wrong don't apply in the absence of government is striking. The argument goes back to the problems of the state of nature. As we've seen, in that condition Hobbes says we're allowed to defend ourselves by whatever means we think helpful. And if we can do anything to help with survival, then there's really nothing that we're not allowed to do. And if there's nothing that's not allowed, then nothing is wrong or unjust.

We can summarize this as follows:

(1) In a state of nature, you're allowed to do anything to help with your survival.
(2) If you're allowed to do anything to help with your survival, then nothing is wrong or unjust.
(3) Therefore, in a state of nature, nothing is wrong or unjust.

This argument is important for Hobbes' theory. If ideas like justice or right and wrong applied in the state of nature, then it could be wrong to impose a social contract on people. After all, if people have rights even without the existence of a government, then we would need to ask whether the imposition of the social contract respects or violates those rights. And if it turns out that such imposition constitutes a violation of rights, then Hobbes can't say that a government's rules are binding simply because they make us better off.

It's not clear that the above argument succeeds. Premise (1) says that people may do anything that helps them with survival. But that seems too strong. Suppose we concede that any possible action could become allowed if it's necessary to survive. It still doesn't follow that everything is allowed all the time. It's one thing to kill a person because you have to in order to stay alive. It's quite another to kill a person just because you feel like it. Even in a state of nature, killing people for fun seems wrong. And it's wrong for the same reasons it's wrong in a society with government: it takes an innocent person's life. It's not wrong just because the law says so.

Hobbes might reply here that the state of nature is so dangerous that we always need to do the most aggressive thing to stay alive. Reason and anticipation tell us to kill preemptively, because every killing of another person is one step closer to safety. Even killing a person in their sleep helps because it takes away a possible threat. But is it really reasonable to say that even a tiny improvement in safety is good enough reason to end someone's life? Can't we be expected to take at least some risk, even a very small risk, before we do such drastic things? Especially when we know that our being hyperaggressive is what makes the state of nature such a horrible place, it seems perfectly reasonable to expect people to avoid such behavior.

Hobbes' claim that a binding social contract can be imposed without agreement is unpromising, then. It requires a conception of morality according to which right and wrong depend entirely on the existence of government and the law. And that's implausible. Once we jettison this conception, however, the question arises whether the imposition of the social contract's terms is morally acceptable. Agreement of some kind remains the most plausible way to answer that question in the affirmative.

ROUSSEAU AND THE GENERAL WILL

Rousseau's *The Social Contract* proposes a different, more ambitious idea of agreement. As discussed in Chapter 3, Rousseau claimed that we're never unfree when we live under the rules of a social contract. Such legislation expresses what Rousseau called the General Will, and that's something with which we can't rationally disagree.

The General Will is a form of everyone's individual wills, combined into a single (and improved) version. It's the will of the public, society as a whole, and unites all of our wills in a way that expresses what we truly want together. This happens, Rousseau argues, because of democratic deliberation. In a democracy, we cannot pass any laws without others agreeing with them. We have to convince them of what we want, and that's going to require appealing to reasons they also share. If I propose a law because it's good for me, but it's bad for you, that will not be acceptable. But if I propose a law that's good for both of us, we may actually agree. As a result, the General Will can't be organized around any one person's individual goals or interests. It can focus only on the common good.

Here's how Rousseau put it:

> There is often a great deal of difference between the will of all and the general will; the latter considers only the common interest, while the former takes private interest into account, and is no more than a sum of particular wills: but take away from these same wills the pluses and minuses that cancel one another, and the general will remains as the sum of the differences.
>
> (Rousseau 1923 [1762]: bk. 2, ch. 3)

Democratic decisions thus reshape all of our individual wants and desires into a single common good. This can happen even if you don't think it's happening. You might face a democratically accepted law that you don't like, perhaps because it happens to be costly for you. Say, the government passes a law raising taxes, and you're none too happy about that. When you're forced to live by this law, you're not forced to do something that goes against your will. Since the law was democratically accepted, it represents your wishes, stripped of those "pluses and minuses" that make you not like higher taxes.

Rousseau's argument presupposes that if we want conflicting things, and the General Will selects one of them, we're not oppressed or coerced in any problematic way when we're forced to go along with that. If the General Will acts on your desire to get tax-funded services, being forced to pay more taxes isn't against your will. This means you agree in the sense required for the social contract.

The argument goes roughly as follows:

(1)   The General Will consists of parts of all our individual wills.
(2)   It's not wrong to force people do to what is part of their own will.
(3)   Therefore, it's not wrong to force people to follow the General Will.

Premise (1) was discussed in Chapter 3. The problem with (1) is that, while the General Will might plausibly be said to represent all our wills if democracies are governed by unanimity rule, no actual democracy can function this way. And once unanimity rule is replaced with something like majority rule, those who are outvoted may not see their wills or wishes represented in the law. In that case, premise (1) seems false.

Premise (2) is questionable also. Rousseau claims that it's not problematic when we're forced to obey the General Will because it tracks part of our own wills. (The part that remains once the "pluses and minuses" have been eliminated.) We can interpret this either as a point about forcing people generally, or as a point about the General Will as a special case.

If intended as a general point about force, Rousseau's claim has to be mistaken. Suppose there's part of me that wants to help you pay off your student loans. And suppose there's another part of me that doesn't. Say, I want to keep the money for my children. If I decide to keep the money, you're not allowed to force me to pay off your loans. This was my decision to make, and I decided otherwise.

The fact that part of me did want to help you is neither here nor there. What matters is that you don't get to choose what part of my will determines my actions. That's up to me, and my decision was that the other part carried the day. You may not like that, and that may be sad. It might even be said that I made the wrong decision, such that the part that wanted to help you should have won. But none of that means you get to override my decision.

Is premise (2) more plausible as a claim about the General Will? Perhaps the General Will is special in that it's okay to force people to follow it, as long as it incorporates at least part of their wills. One possible reason would be that accepting the General Will is just part of life in a democracy. And if we have to accept certain laws as expressions of the General Will, then we can't expect to live under only laws that we each fully agree with. We have to compromise, and if the laws at least represent part of what we want, maybe that's enough to say they're acceptable to us all. It certainly beats having laws we completely reject.

This special argument is convincing only if we indeed must live with others under a single set of (democratic) laws. Only then must we accept whatever laws we agree on with others. But if we're free to live by our own lights, there's no need to accept such compromises. And if there's no such need, then it can't be said that forcing us to accept them constitutes no wrong. But this, of course, raises the question whether we really must live together under a single government. The General Will itself cannot show that this is true. The General Will is the output of democratic decision-making. But the decision to live under democratic rule in the first place cannot itself be democratically made. Or at least, it cannot be democratically made without raising the same question again: why is that prior democratic decision to accept democratic decisions binding? And so on.

Of course, thinkers like Hobbes and Rousseau strongly believe we must live in political society. And they may be right that life in society is vastly preferable to life in a state of nature. But that wasn't our question. The question was whether people can be *rightfully forced* to accept the rules of society, and the social contract was supposed to supply the answer. Rousseau's theory doesn't give us that answer. In order to accept his theory, we first have to accept that it's legitimate to impose laws on people. But the social contract was supposed to show that this is legitimate. We're back to where we started.

JUSTICE AND THE SOCIAL CONTRACT

Let's set these concerns aside and look more closely at how the social contract is supposed to work. The point of social contract theory is that everyone must follow the rules. Which rules? The ones we can all agree on. This agreement, even if only hypothetical, constrains which rules and laws can count as legitimate. For Hobbes, the constraint was that laws must keep us safe. The delivery of safety replaces agreement, for Hobbes. For Rousseau, laws have to be democratically acceptable. Such acceptability is as good as actual agreement.

Several other constraints can be derived from the idea that rules must be acceptable to all. It's generally thought, for example, that various basic liberal rights would be accepted. Rights of freedom of movement, assembly, religion, and political participation would be accepted by everyone. And the same is true about various bodily rights and the freedom to choose your work. Beyond this, however, there is much disagreement among social contract theorists. Some argue that rules acceptable to all must seriously reduce material inequality in society. Others think that disagreement about inequality is too deep to come up with an acceptable rule, and so government may simply have to stay out of many such issues.[2]

Social contract theory treats rules of justice and morality as social creations. They're the things that have to be accepted by society before they're binding. Morality and justice are not given to us as if from some external force, whether that be God, nature, the universe, or something else. Ideas of right and wrong are human creations, norms accepted by people in society because they help us live together better. Contract theorists like Hobbes and Rousseau thus reject any notion of moral or natural rights. Such rights would have to exist prior to or independent of the social contract, and the entire point of the social contract is to generate these rights. Hobbes summarized it as follows: "Justice and Propriety begin with the constitution of Common-wealth" (Hobbes 1997 [1651]: ch. XV).

One argument in favor of this approach is that we can't live together very well unless we adopt some shared understanding of justice and morality. We all have different ideas about what's really right, what justice really requires. And if we live together with people who disagree with us, we can do one of two things. We can try to force our own ideas on others, making them accept what we think we know is truly right and good. Or we can try to find some shared understanding of what's right, and live by that. The social contract aims for the latter, of course. And that means we must sometimes accept rules we wouldn't have thought were right if we were living by ourselves.[3] As Hobbes put it:

> For in the differences of private men, to declare what is Equity, what is Justice, and what is morall Vertue, and to make them binding, there is need of the Ordinances of Soveraign Power, and Punishments to be ordained for such as shall break them; which Ordinances are therefore part of the Civill Law.
>
> (Hobbes 1997 [1651]: ch. XXVI)

This is a very attractive idea, perhaps the greatest virtue of social contract theory. At the same time, it can have some troubling implications. Crucial to this approach is that socially accepted rules are individually binding, meaning that when our personal judgment conflicts with the rules of the social contract, those rules take priority. But objections to social rules can seem very pressing. Social rules can be discriminatory, unfair, oppressive. As in the case of Socrates, they can cost you your life. In those cases, we'll want to know why we must follow the rules, rather than do (what we think is) the right thing.

Perhaps it might be said that such rules are actually not binding, say, because they violate the constraints imposed by the idea of a social contract, treating people unequally or the like. Perhaps no one would accept a contract that could cost you your life (although Socrates said he did accept those terms). But even if this argument works for some rules, it cannot work for all unjust or unfair rules. We're invoking here a sense of justice or fairness that's independent of the social contract, and we're invoking it to judge whether or not rules are binding. But that move is simply not available to the social contract theorist. The entire point of social contract theory is that social rules must override such individual judgments, even when those judgments strike us as very clearly right.

The most promising reply by social contract theorists refers to an idea called civil disobedience. To engage in civil disobedience is to disobey the law in a particular way, and with a specific aim. The aim of law breaking in this manner is to *reform* the law. When we disobey in that way, and with that specific aim, the law need not be taken as definitively binding, according to this idea.

Typically, civil disobedience is said to require the following things:

(1) Disobedience is openly done, perhaps even publicly announced, in order to draw attention to the mistaken law.
(2) Disobedience must be non-violent and not disrupt public order.
(3) Punishment for breaking the law must be readily accepted.

Done this way, the argument goes, one can break the law while still maintaining one's allegiance to the rules of society (Rawls 1999 [1971]: 319–22). One is breaking the law, but not thereby announcing readiness to put one's judgment above the rules of society. Instead, breaking the law in this manner is a kind of performative act, a way of drawing public attention to problematic rules in society, with the hope of thereby making things better.

A classic example of civil disobedience is the American minister and Civil Rights activist Martin Luther King's (1929–1968) 1963 protest in Birmingham, Alabama. King was arrested after he protested against racial injustice without permission from the authorities. In his *Letter from a Birmingham Jail*, King justified his actions and outlined his theory of civil disobedience. According to King, if lawbreakers follow the requirements above, they don't deny that the rules of society are binding. All they do is deny that unjust laws, such as those upholding racial segregation, are binding. As a result, King said, one can disobey the law while also accepting the rules of society (King 1963).

The theory of civil disobedience is important. And it may be true, if we follow its requirements, that we can permissibly disobey laws even if we have a general moral obligation to obey. However, this doesn't solve the problem we're facing. That problem is that the social contract supposedly determines what counts as just or unjust, and the terms of that contract can include highly objectionable social rules and laws. In those cases, the problem isn't merely that we're not morally allowed to *disobey* those laws. The problem is that those laws or rules can't even *count* as unjust in the first place. Even if we're morally allowed to disobey, in the manner outlined by the theory of civil disobedience, we can't disobey because the law is unjust.

But that's just bizarre. Injustice is *the* prime legitimate reason for breaking the law. And the idea of a social contract theory threatens to take that away. We might have other reasons for not liking the law, say because it's not even-handed, inefficient, or insulting. But those reasons don't fully capture the situation in which people like Martin Luther King find themselves. Their situation is one of injustice, not (only) those other reasons. Indeed, injustice was the reason King offered for his disobedience in his *Letter*. The idea of a social contract means King was simply mistaken in offering this argument. And that remains problematic.

QUESTIONS

(1) Do you think we have a social contract in our society? How can we know what it says?

(2) The social contract doesn't require actual agreement. Are there other situations in which we can ignore whether people actually agree to being treated in certain (forceful) ways? Is there a difference?

(3) Suppose we agree that there's so much disagreement that we can't all follow our own rules. Imagine now that we also disagree about what the rules of the social contract say. How can we resolve that disagreement?

NOTES

1 The reference is to the police tactic of splitting up people suspected of committing a crime together and offering them sentence reductions in exchange for incriminating evidence about their partner. The idea being that it's in the collective interest of the suspects to keep their mouths shut, but in each of their individual interests to turn in the other. The intended result (by the police, at least) is that both suspects talk, and so end up convicted.

2 A good discussion of this is Gaus (2010).

3 The strongest statement comes from Kant: "The legislative authority can belong only to the united will of the people. For since all right is to proceed from it, it *cannot* do anyone wrong by its law" (Kant 2017 [1797]: 6:313). And: "a people has a duty to put up with even what is held to be an unbearable abuse of supreme authority" (Kant 2017 [1797]: 6:320).

JUSTICE

Justice is a central concept in politics. When we consider the role of government in our lives, the first thing we want is for it to be just.[1] The main branches of government are supposed to uphold, enforce, and promote justice. And, importantly, they're not to perpetrate any injustices themselves. We turn to the police and courts when we're looking for justice. We expect law enforcement to deliver just results, and to deliver them in a manner that's just as well. It's no coincidence that we call these parts of government "the justice system."

In *Crito*, Socrates asked whether he should obey the law. That question arose because the lawgivers of Athens were treating him unjustly. Socrates was facing the death penalty despite being innocent. And it's a paradigmatic injustice to punish the innocent. In light of that injustice, we wonder whether Socrates should obey. That question doesn't come up if a law or verdict is just.

To say that a law or government is unjust, then, is to say something very serious. As *Crito* illustrates, it's to indict it in a way so significant as to call into question basic political ideas like authority and obedience. At the same time, determining what justice means is not so simple. People disagree – and disagree vehemently – about what's just and unjust. To make some progress, let's begin with the basics.

DOI: 10.4324/9781003250692-6

JUSTICE: THE BASICS

Justice is a basic moral category, delineating our most import-ant ideas of right and wrong. Aristotle distinguished between two different branches: distributive and corrective justice. *Distributive justice* tells us what people are due, in the sense that their not having it would be unjust. *Corrective justice* responds to unjust misallocations, situations in which people do not have what they're due (Aristotle 1999: 1130b).

Distributive justice is prior to corrective justice. We first need to know what people are due before we can know whether what they have needs correcting. Distributive justice tells us about the rights and liberties, as well as the duties and responsibilities, we have. This concerns the distribution of stuff, such as the rightful ownership of physical possessions and claims to income and wealth. But distributive justice also con-cerns other things, such as the rights we have over our bodies, whether we are free to choose our job, whether we're free to engage in religious worship, what we owe to others, and whether governments can interfere with our possessions and freedoms or force us to do things.[2]

Justice requires that such rights and freedoms be respected and upheld. When political or legal institutions misallocate these, say, by denying rights or freedoms that we ought to enjoy, that calls for rectification. Corrective justice is about how to rectify such problems. It concerns how resources and opportunities might have to be redistributed in response to an unfair allocation. It tells us whether we need to simply repair the allocation, putting in people's hands what rightfully belongs to them, or whether we may have to do more, such as offering the victims of injustice additional compensation. Corrective justice also informs the appropriate response to wrongdoing, such as what might be the correct way to impose punishments or penalties on those who commit injustice.

Not everything that's right or wrong is also just or unjust. Sometimes things are right, but it's not a concern of justice.

At other times things may be wrong, without also being unjust. This is possible even when things are very seriously wrong. Some of the most hurtful things people can do will not rise to the level of injustice. If you cheat on your spouse after many years of faithful marriage, that's a serious wrong and may well be devastating. But it's not an injustice. The wrong in question here is of a different kind.

Ideas about distributive justice have changed over time. Ancient philosophers wrote about justice as a virtue, suggesting that it's primarily a character trait. To them, justice is something we do, a disposition to treat others in ways that give them their due. On this approach, justice is thoroughly interpersonal, meaning that whenever an injustice occurs, there will be someone committing it. Early modern authors saw things differently, considering justice as primarily consisting of a set of rules, specifically those rules that are essential to life in society. These prohibit us from harming one another through violence, theft, or fraud, require that we keep our contracts, and so on.

More recently, justice has become increasingly associated with the role of government in society, as something that requires a public authority in order to be achieved. Justice is sometimes thought of as *social* justice now, meaning that it obtains only or primarily within societies and speaks to how societies are internally ordered. Theories of social justice, for instance, are often heavily concerned with reducing material inequality within a society, while remaining relatively unconcerned about inequalities around the world.

These modern conceptions see an important connection between justice and government. Justice and injustice are not mere private matters. These are not simply wrongs between you and me, say. Justice is a *public concern* – it involves the kinds of rights and wrongs where third parties may be involved. More precisely, justice concerns the rights and wrongs for which society as a whole and, by extension, the powers of government may be involved.[3] To say something is a matter of justice is to open the door to coercion and punishment. It's an issue where it could make sense to call the cops. In this sense, talk of justice raises the stakes. The same isn't true of things that are wrong but not unjust.

Justice obtains when no publicly correctable or enforceable wrongs exist. In those cases, everyone enjoys what, as a matter of distributive justice, they are due. And when we all enjoy what we're due, there is no job for corrective justice to do. In that sense, justice is as much about the *absence of injustice* as the achievement of some overall outcome or goal.

HUME AND THE CIRCUMSTANCES OF JUSTICE

The Scottish philosopher David Hume (1711–1776) argued that justice is not a natural phenomenon. It's not something that we find, as if it were out there as a part of nature. Rather, justice is a set of rules that humans create when they live together. In particular, these are rules that we find help us live together better.

One of Hume's arguments for this view is that justice only makes sense under certain conditions. Justice is something that arises only when (a) there's enough stuff for all of us to live, but not so much that we all naturally have everything we want or need, and (b) we human beings are selfish enough that we don't want to care or work for others like we do for ourselves.[4]

Let's make this a little more precise. (a) If there weren't enough for everyone to survive, then justice wouldn't be possible. If we're both in a shipwreck and the only raft available can save just one of us, there's no just or fair solution. It's no more just that you get to live while I must die than the reverse.[5] By contrast, if there were more than enough to go around, justice wouldn't be needed. If nature provided so much that we could simply reach for what we wanted, we wouldn't worry about who owns what. Justice would be superfluous in that case, as there'd be no need for rules that settle who owns what. There are no police in the Garden of Eden.

(b) The same would be true if we were all happy to care for others as we do for ourselves. In that case, we wouldn't have to worry about scarcity. Whenever you were hungry, you'd just ask your neighbor to cook you a meal. And being altruistic, they'd provide you with food. But that's not how we are. We're happy to work for our own meals, and we're happy to help others some of the time. But we don't work for others the same way that we take care of ourselves.

And so, Hume concluded that: "'tis only from the selfishness and confin'd generosity of men, along with the scanty provision nature has made for his wants, that justice derives its origin" (Hume 1978 [1739]: bk. 3, pt. 2, sec. 2).

Because nature has made only such "scanty provision," and because we're all at least somewhat selfish, there's only enough for all of us to live and satisfy our needs if we're willing to put in the work, but if we are, we should all be able to live well. But this means there's a real question about who owns what, who gets to enjoy the fruits of our labors, and how to deal with situations in which we want the same thing but cannot all have it. Solving this issue is what the rules of justice are for. It's a way of settling and preventing the conflicts that can result from having competing interests and conditions of scarcity.

This offers a useful way of thinking about what justice requires. In order to solve the kind of material scarcity that can be overcome by human efforts, the rules of justice must help us cooperate and live together in ways that achieve this goal. This means that living with justice must be good for us, in material terms. It must leave us better off than we'd be without it. And since we expect everyone to follow the rules of justice, this must be true for all of us. As Hume put it, when we think about life with justice, we must all find ourselves "a gainer, on balancing the account" (Hume 1978 [1739]: bk. 3, pt. 2, sec. 2). Justice serves our mutual advantage.

The first and most important step toward achieving such mutual advantage is to establish a "stability of possessions." By this, Hume meant that people get to keep their stuff, specifically the stuff they produce themselves or acquire from others by agreement. This stability of possessions is key because, without it, we'd all be tempted to grab what others have or make. And that would mean no one would want to work anymore, as producing valuable things would only make you a target. That would not benefit anyone. Even the most successful thief would soon run out of things to steal. Justice thus requires that we respect people's rights over their property.

Second, justice must facilitate interactions that are *mutually advantageous*, interactions that leave people better off than they would have been in the absence of justice. One important thing this requires is that contracts are protected. Contracts facilitate exchange, allowing people to enter into transactions they see as to their benefit. Contractual exchanges allow us to swap the things we possess for things that we'd like to possess but are currently held by others. When both parties want such a swap, the exchange will render them both better off. Justice, therefore, requires that contracts be upheld.

Of course, doing what's just can be inconvenient. Saying that justice is to our mutual advantage doesn't deny that. If I have bills to pay, it would be easy for me to just steal some money from your wallet and use that to pay them. But doing so would violate Hume's idea of the stability of possessions, and thus be unjust. I will have to do the inconvenient thing and work for my money myself. Still, living with rules that require that we respect each other's possessions is much better overall than living without such rules, and we can all see this. Because we understand this arrangement as a happy one, at least as long as others also respect it, we'll uphold the rules of justice (Hume 1978 [1739]: bk. 3, pt. 2, sec. 2).

Hume's ideas about justice have some plausible implications. If Hume is right, for example, justice is self-reinforcing. It's something we can all understand is beneficial, and for that reason want to keep going. Hume offers an analogy of two people rowing in a boat. Each pull of the oars is inconvenient, but if we do it together, we get where we want to go.

This means we'll want to keep pulling together. And we'll resent others when they stop, just like we resent people who commit injustices. The implication is that ubiquitous enforcement is not necessary – we don't need a police officer on every street corner. Most people, most of the time, will want to do the right thing. And they'll do it because they see that if everyone follows the rules, things work much better. This seems correct.[6]

But Hume's theory raises some questions, too. If justice is a human solution to problems that arise from certain circumstances, then there could also be circumstances in which nothing is unjust. Perhaps this is plausible in situations like the one where two people have to fight over a single raft. Still, it's a very strong claim to say that there exist circumstances in which no action could be unjust. The American philosopher Judith Jarvis Thomson (1929–2020) observed that it's a necessary truth that one ought not to torture babies to death for fun. By this she meant that there's simply no world we can imagine in which torturing babies to death for fun is okay. It's not only true that doing this is wrong, but it couldn't be not true (Thomson 1990: 18).

Thomson's point seems clearly correct. But that just means it's always, under all circumstances, wrong to torture babies to death for fun. The wrongness here makes this act a prime candidate for an injustice. It's a gross violation of a person's rights over their body, even if they're only a baby. And violations of such rights are paradigmatic examples of injustice. Contrary to Hume's theory, then, it seems that at least some parts of justice are not sensitive to circumstance.

Hume might accept Thomson's point. In his discussion, he draws a distinction between the "natural" and "artificial" parts of morality. Justice is artificial because it has to be developed in human society, and it almost entirely concerns rules about material possessions. The natural parts of morality include rights and wrongs that involve our bodies. The distinction has to do with psychology. We begin to care about justice only after we see that it performs a useful function for us, according to Hume, and this makes it artificial. But violations of our persons, we care about naturally. If what's naturally wrong in that sense also could not fail to be wrong, such that we psychologically couldn't help but care about those violations, then Hume might agree with Thomson's point.

JUSTICE AND OWNERSHIP

Hume's distinction restricts the term "justice" to material concerns, like property and contract. Those are matters of justice, according to Hume, and therefore conventional creations of human society (as opposed to naturally existing things). Other rights-claims, like our rights over our persons, are not part of justice, defined this way. This a perfectly fine way of using the term justice, of course. (The meaning of words is of little philosophical consequence.) And it's certainly more plausible to say that rules of ownership depend on the circumstances of society than that all rights do.

Still, even this weaker position is disputed. In his discussion of property rights, John Locke argued that we cannot so neatly separate the rights we have over our persons from the rights we have over our material possessions. Locke's argument is straightforward:

> every Man has a *Property* in his own *Person.* This no Body has any Right to but himself. The *Labour* of his Body, and the *Work* of his Hands, we may say, are properly his. Whatsoever then he removes out of the State that Nature hath provided, and left it in, hath mixed his *Labour* with, and joined to it something that is his own, and thereby makes it his *Property*.
>
> (Locke 1988 [1689]: II, 27)

Locke's argument starts from the idea that we have rights over our persons. And those rights, Locke observes, are very much like rights of ownership. At their core, these are rights to exclude others from unwanted use. In that sense, you own yourself. But if you own yourself, then you also own the things you do. Control over your body requires control over the work you do using that body. The implication, Locke argues, is that you own the things you produce through your own work.

We can summarize this argument as follows:

(1) You own your person, including your body.
(2) Owning your body means owning the labor you perform using your body.
(3) Therefore, you own your labor.
(4) If you own your labor, then you must also own the product of your labor, at least when you work on something that's not owned by others.
(5) Therefore, you own the things you produce, at least when you worked on something that was not owned by others.

Premise (1) is a version of Thomson's point that we have strong rights over our selves. Premise (2) is an implication of that point. If both are true, then (3) must also be true. Premise (4) is often called Locke's labor-mixing argument. As Locke suggests in the quotation above, if you "mix" your labor with something unowned, then you come to own that thing.

Consider an example. Suppose we live in a situation without laws or rules about ownership, and you come across a log. You'd like a canoe, to help you with fishing, and spend several days carving a canoe out of that log. Suppose now that I come along and see that useful canoe. If I take the canoe, I'd clearly be taking something that belongs to you. And the reason it belongs to you is also clear: you made it.

Although this idea is very plausible, the labor-mixing argument has turned out to be extremely controversial. Locke's argument seems to rely on the general idea that if you mix something you own with something that's unowned, then you come to own that unowned thing. But as a general idea, that has to be false. As the American philosopher Robert Nozick (1938–2002), who generally accepted Locke's view, pointed out, it's clearly not always true that we come to own unowned things if we mix something we own with them. If you own a can of tomato juice and mix it with the ocean, which is unowned, you don't thereby acquire an ocean. You lose the juice (Nozick 2003 [1974]: 174–5).

Locke's point, then, cannot rely on this general principle about the logic of mixing. But Locke doesn't present it as such. He presents it as a point about control over your person and, by extension, labor. To have such control requires having control over the things you do. That includes your work, and the products of your work. The idea is that our actions have a certain outward orientation. We don't just carve a log; we carve it to get a canoe. If someone takes away the canoe, they take away the very point of your action. That's as good as taking your action. This is why Locke thinks that if you don't get to control the product of your labor, you don't really control your labor. And if you don't really control your labor, you don't really control yourself.

This argument doesn't deny that ownership can be conventional. Societies may have different rules about how the contours of property claims are defined, such as what counts as the kind of nuisance or pollution that infringes property rights, after how long owners lose their rights over an abandoned piece of property, and what the terms of intellectual property are. It just denies that ownership is entirely conventional. It's one thing to say that ownership has a conventional element, quite another to say that the very idea of ownership has to be invented. Locke denies the latter, but not the former.

If Locke is right, then our rights over our bodies are not so separate from our rights over our stuff. To respect someone as a person, we have to respect both their body and their possessions. And if that's true, and Thomson is correct that our rights over our bodies do not depend on circumstances, then Hume must have been wrong to say that justice depends on circumstances.

This is so even if we restrict the meaning of justice to material concerns. The upshot is that justice is not "artificial" but "natural," in Hume's terms. This is the theory of natural rights. These contrast with conventional rights.

But many worry about the implications of this position. The rights Thomson discusses are quite strong. You have no right to use my body without my permission. And this is true even if you really badly desire, or even need, access to my body. If somehow the only way you can stay alive is to have one of my kidneys, but I don't want to give you one, I can deny you access to my kidney. Perhaps I'd be selfish to say no, but neither you nor anyone else can force me to donate a kidney.[7]

If Locke is right, then we might have to conclude that we have similarly strong rights over our possessions. Even if you need access to my property to survive, then, I would have the right to reject you. But that's just not true. If you need to get to the hospital in order to live, and taking my car is the only way to get there, you can surely take it. And you can take it even if I say that you're not allowed to. Perhaps you will have to pay me compensation for taking my car, and you certainly should pay for whatever damage you might cause. But it's clear that you were morally permitted to do what you did.

By extension, many people think we can justly be taxed for various worthy purposes. It's commonly accepted that we can be taxed in order to fight material inequality, to fund public services like museums or schools, to build roads, to maintain a military apparatus, and so on. But it's not okay to make people support those things through forced labor. And so, the analogy between rights over our persons and rights over our possessions just doesn't seem as tight as Locke makes it out to be. This is a significant problem for the labor–mixing account.

There may be room in Locke's theory to resolve this. If we interpret Locke's theory as not so much about mixing, but about protecting our labor in order to protect control over ourselves, then we can ask how much our labor needs to be protected in order to achieve such control. It may be that, while control over our bodies has to be near absolute, weaker protections of our labor would still provide us with sufficient control over ourselves. That might allow for things like taxation while not undercutting rights over our bodies.

JOHN RAWLS, *A THEORY OF JUSTICE*

How exactly to thread that needle, making enough space for things like plausible taxation or emergency use of others' property, while also giving people real control over their lives, remains a very difficult question. And Locke's argument doesn't offer much guidance on how to answer it. One way of answering it is to think about all of our rights and duties in a more systematic manner.

John Rawls, in his influential book, *A Theory of Justice* (Rawls 1999 [1971]), offers such an answer. Rawls proposed a model for thinking about justice using the idea of a social contract. Just as the social contract says that rules of law are whatever the people together accept, so too can we understand the rules of morality and justice, Rawls suggested. What's just or unjust is whatever is acceptable to all of us, at least insofar as we're thinking rationally and impartially. To Rawls, if we make sure that justice is acceptable in this way, we can be sure that its rules are good for us and treat everyone fairly.

Rawls devised a method for formulating what these principles look like. This method imagines people as equally positioned bargainers, negotiating over which rules would determine what counts as justice between people. This bargaining situation he called the *Original Position*. It's an imaginary exercise that we can use to ask whether rules are truly acceptable to us all. The idea behind the Original Position is that if people are fairly situated, and use all and only relevant information, then the rules to which they agree will also be fair.

The rules that are chosen in the Original Position will be beneficial and impartial, Rawls argued. Such rules must be beneficial because we must be rationally motivated to accept them. The rules will be impartial because, in Rawls' account, we choose them from behind a *Veil of Ignorance*, a device that removes certain types of information from our choice. Specifically, it obscures information about our own particular characteristics, such as whether we're male or female, our racial background, whether or not we're religious, whether we're young or old, and so on. This means we won't choose rules to benefit some at the expense of others. Once the Veil is lifted, we might turn out to be one of those persons who pay the cost, and no one would take that risk.

Rawls argued that people so situated would select two principles of justice. In simplified form, these hold:[8]

(1)   Each person has an equal right to the most extensive total system of equal basic liberties, compatible with a similar system of liberty for all.
(2)   Social or economic inequalities are acceptable only insofar as they are both:

    a.   to the greatest benefit of the least advantaged, and
    b.   attached to offices and positions open to all.

The first of these principles concerns personal, social, and political rights. The second concerns economic rights. Let's take them in turn.

The first principle tells us which basic rights and liberties we have. This includes personal and political rights such as rights over our bodies, freedom of association, expression and religion, the right to vote, to hold public office, and to be treated in accordance with the rule of law, and so on. Rawls argued that the only principle that's rationally and impartially acceptable is one that gives us all as much of these rights and freedoms as is possible, consistent with the same freedoms for all. The argument is straightforward. We each want more rather than less of these freedoms. And not knowing who we are in society, because of the Veil of Ignorance, the only choice is to select the greatest freedom we can all enjoy together.

Where the first principle requires maximal equal personal and political freedom, the second principle is quite different. This principle concerns economic goods, and it allows inequality. Its two requirements are that the positions or jobs that lead to such inequalities must be open to everyone, and, famously, that such inequalities must maximally improve the prospects of society's least well off. Rational and impartial people would allow such inequalities, Rawls argued. Imagine a choice between two societies you might live in. Society A is perfectly equal with a certain standard of living for everyone. Society B is unequal, but everyone's standard of living, including the poor, is higher than that of Society A. The rational choice then is to select B.

Rawls' insight is that there are differences between how certain rights and freedoms work. Some rights are zero-sum, in the sense that more for one means less for others. Political influence is an example, at least for a given population. If I get more votes in an election, that means my political influence goes up and your relative political influence goes down. This kind of influence is a little like a pie of fixed size, and the larger my slice becomes, the smaller yours will be.

But economic life isn't zero-sum. Societies can be richer or poorer, and ones that enforce material equality tend to be (much) poorer. Societies with market economies might allow quite a bit of inequality, but they are also places in which everyone is much better off, and that includes, especially, the poor.[9] Here, it's like the size of the pie changes depending on how we slice it. If we insist that everyone gets equal-sized slices, the pie will be small, and each of our slices will be small as well. If we allow that some get bigger slices than others, the pie grows, even the smallest slices are bigger than the equal slices, and we can all eat more pie. Knowing this, Rawls argued, people in the Original Position will choose to allow economic inequality.

This idea has proven very influential. Very few philosophers now believe that justice requires strict material equality.

That said, Rawls' account of how just much inequality justice allows is controversial. Rawls wanted to limit inequality as much as possible. That's the point of the first qualification of the second principle, (2a) what Rawls called the *Difference Principle*. This principle allows inequality only insofar as it benefits society's least well off. Rawls' suggestion is that if you don't know who you'll be, because of the Veil of Ignorance, it's rational to maximize your worst possible outcome. Rational and impartial choosers will thus allow inequalities to the extent that these improve the position of the worst off, and no more. If so, the Difference Principle follows.

However, it's not clear that this is indeed the rational choice. Consider three possible societies, with three possible groups in which you might end up. Let the numbers represent economic goods we care about, with more being better than less. You choose between these societies, not knowing whether you'll be in Group 1, 2, or 3.

	Society A	*Society B*	*Society C*
Group 1	35	120	80
Group 2	35	65	50
Group 3	35	40	45

A commitment to strict equality would require that we choose Society A. But surely no one would choose A in this situation. Such a preference would be irrational, since every group in B and C does better than all groups in A. The Difference Principle recommends Society C, as that's the best outcome for Group 3, the least well-off. But why should we prioritize this outcome so much? Society C seems quite attractive, promising a life in which we're much better off if we're in either Group 1 or Group 2, while only slightly worse off if we're Group 3. Given this choice, picking B over C seems like a worthy gamble. It involves a slight risk for one-third of our possible outcomes, to get much better prospects for two-thirds of them.

Rawls said that if we do not know which group we'll end up being in, it's rational to make sure the worst possible outcome is the best it can be. But this does not seem correct. Standard rational choice theory holds that situations like this call for maximizing the average outcome (that is, choose the highest number that results from adding up all outcomes and dividing them by three) (Harsanyi 1975). Or perhaps it's rational to maximize the average, subject to the constraint that the worst possible result isn't disastrous (Kavka 1986: 142–3). Either way, in the choice above, Society B is selected. But Society B contains more inequality than the Difference Principle allows.

Rawls described the intuition behind the Difference Principle as follows: "The intuitive idea is that the social order is not to establish and secure the more attractive prospects of those better off unless doing so is to the advantage of those less fortunate" (Rawls 1999 [1971]: 65).

This evokes Hume's idea that justice is for mutual advantage. Justice requires that all parts of society benefit from economic activity, and it prohibits some benefiting at the expense of others. As Rawls writes early in the book, "it is not just that some should have less in order that others may prosper" (Rawls 1999 [1971]: 13). And we should be especially cognizant of this when considering society's least well-off, as they are most likely to made to bear burdens for the benefit of others.

The Difference Principle, however, goes one step further. It interprets Hume's idea as requiring that, unless inequalities *maximally benefit* the least well off, they come *at the expense* of the least well off. But that's not at all obvious. A choice that results in one group not receiving their best possible outcome need not be a choice that comes at that group's expense. Consider again the example above. The choice between Societies B or C is between a choice between benefiting Groups 1 and 2 or benefiting Group 3. We can't say that choosing Society B (benefiting Groups 1 and 2) comes at the expense of Group 3, unless we also say that choosing Society C (benefiting Group 3) comes at the expense of Groups 1 and 2.

Rawls' Difference Principle rules out the former, but not the latter choice. And that means it's privileging the position of the least well-off, so that their not receiving the maximum possible benefit does come at their expense, but other groups not receiving the same does not come at their expense. But we lack an argument for this. It's not clear why one group's non-maximal benefit does violate Hume's idea about justice as mutual advantage, while another group's does not. A theory of justice that models people as equals, as parties endowed with equal bargaining power, may well be inconsistent with this.[10]

Still, whether or not the Difference Principle is the best way of capturing the overarching Humean idea, Rawls' contribution remains important. Spelling out and capturing this intuition in the first place represent significant progress in our understanding of justice. What exactly justice requires for a society to live up to that idea is a further question.

JUSTICE AND RIGHTS

Benefiting one group at the expense of another is unacceptable as a matter of justice. This is true even if the former group is much larger than the latter. It's true even if the latter consists of a single person. Justice is individualistic in this sense. It protects every individual against being made to serve the demands of society or the state. We each first and foremost get to live our own lives.

Let's turn again to Rawls for a succinct statement of the point:

> Each person possesses an inviolability founded on justice that even the welfare of society as a whole cannot override. For this reason justice denies that the loss of freedom for some is made right by a greater good shared by others.
>
> (Rawls 1999 [1971]: 3)

According to Rawls, people are inviolable because we're separate. This separateness of persons stems from the idea that we each have but one life to live, and so we all have to live our own lives. From each of our own point of view, even the welfare of society as a whole doesn't compensate for individual losses. If that societal welfare doesn't somehow accrue to us, the costs we are made to bear for it are just that: costs. Justice protects us as individuals from having such losses imposed on us.

Rawls introduced this idea of the separateness of persons as part of a critique of the theory of utilitarianism. Utilitarians hold that which actions are right is determined by two things. First, we must do whatever has the best consequences. Second, consequences are better or worse based on how much happiness they produce overall. As John Stuart Mill, perhaps the theory's greatest defender, put it, this leads to a very simple ethical rule: "[A]ctions are right in proportion as they tend to promote happiness, wrong as they tend to produce the reverse of happiness" (Mill 2002 [1861]: ch. 2).

Utilitarianism is plausible in many contexts, especially government. It's often true that policies that create more happiness overall are a good idea. And it's common to evaluate policy proposals by doing a kind of cost-benefit analysis. Such an analysis adds up the good and bad effects of a policy, effectively asking the same thing that utilitarianism asks: will this, on balance, make society happier?

The utilitarian calculation of overall happiness allows for various trade-offs. It allows that some people may be made less happy if that's outweighed by the happiness of others (either because there are enough of them or because, even for a smaller group, they become happier by enough). Rawls thought this was unacceptable. It's fine for a single person to make trade-offs within his or her own single life. We may forgo happiness today in order to be happier later in life. But trading off one person's happiness for another's is quite a different thing. To do so seems to imply that people matter only insofar as their happiness feeds into the overall utility calculation. They don't merit any special consideration, respect, or standing. Utilitarianism thus fails to take people seriously enough as individuals (Rawls 1999 [1971]: 24).

Rawls' worry is about justice. He didn't say that Mill was mistaken to argue that things get better when we produce more happiness overall. They very well may. His point was that justice isn't only about making things better. It's also about *how* we make them better. Making things better by sacrificing some for the benefit of others is simply not allowed. No amount of overall happiness can overcome that transgression.

Consider an example. Imagine a society plagued by police corruption. The government wants to crack down, but is having a hard time finding the guilty cops. The people in society, however, think the government just isn't really taking the problem seriously – perhaps they're protecting their own, perhaps they, too, are corrupt. Social unrest has gotten so serious that several protests have devolved into violence and rioting, with innocent people getting harmed. Suppose now someone proposes the following. If we can't find cops that are actually guilty, here's an old cranky cop with no friends. Let's fabricate some evidence and arrest him, to give the impression that the government is addressing the problem. Things will calm down, faith in government will be restored, and everyone will be much happier. (Everyone except that cop, of course.)

Clearly, it would be unjust to convict or even arrest the cop. Cranky and friendless he may be, but guilty he's not, and justice doesn't allow convicting the innocent. The utilitarian, however, might have to consider convicting the cop. As long as enough happiness were gained by convicting the old crank, doing so might be the right thing. That would require a lot of happiness, enough to outweigh the misery visited upon him (and perhaps the additional unrest that would occur if the story got out). But if the happiness gained would be enough, the utilitarian must say it would be right to convict an innocent man.

The problem is clear, of course. Justice protects us as individuals, using rights as its main tool. And even old cranks have rights. Rights shield us from having to do or undergo unwanted things and give us freedom to live by our own lights. That includes having burdens, even socially useful burdens, placed on us. To force the old crank to bear the burdens of police corruption would be wrong. It treats him as a mere resource for others, and justice doesn't allow that. The inviolability of persons, manifested by our rights, stands in the way.

Utilitarians disagree with Rawls' objection, of course. According to Mill, utilitarianism can recognize individual rights and the crucial role they play in justice. Mill saw justice as a set of protections that society ought to give us because having those protections is generally conducive to happiness[11] (Mill 2002 [1861]: ch. 5). And one thing that makes people very nervous and unhappy is living in a place where rights don't mean much. Thus, even if we can create a lot of happiness by violating someone's rights, the better course of action will be to refrain from doing so. In the long run, that will create much more happiness overall.

This response raises questions of its own. Sure, a rule that requires respect for people's rights leads to more happiness than a rule that denies rights altogether. But what about a rule that requires that we respect rights except when a single breach has enormous happiness benefits, at the cost of only one unwilling individual? Such situations might come up very rarely, and so this rule might not create much unrest. (Alternatively, we could keep the rule a secret.) So, this may be even more happiness–producing than Mill's proposal.

If so, the utilitarian would again seem committed to sacrificing innocent individuals for the greater good. But this means that under utilitarianism nothing is *in principle* excluded from justice, including using people in such ways. And that's inconsistent with what Rawls saw as the fundamental idea of justice. It simply doesn't take our rights seriously enough.

QUESTIONS

(1) In societies like ours, when we seek justice, we look to the police and the courts. Why are those the first places we look?

(2)   Can you imagine circumstances under which justice would require something very different from what it requires today? What is it about those circumstances that changes things that way?

(3)   Does the existence of economic inequality mean that some are benefiting at the expense of others? Does this depend on how much inequality there is, or something else?

NOTES

1   In one of the more famous sentences of twentieth-century political philosophy, John Rawls wrote: "Justice is the first virtue of social institutions" (Rawls 1999 [1971]: 3).

2   Rights can play different roles. Sometimes, rights protect our freedom or ability to do something, such as the right to freedom of movement. These are often called *liberty-rights* (or *privileges*). At other times, rights (or *claim-rights*) mean that we are *owed* something. If you and I sign a contract, I can have the right that you deliver certain goods. Such rights are fulfilled by other people complying with an obligation (here, the obligation to deliver what was contracted). At yet other times, our rights give us the ability (or *power*) to make certain legal or moral changes to our (other) rights or obligations. The right to sell your car is your ability to transfer ownership of the car to a willing buyer. Finally, rights can protect us from others making such changes to our rights. The right to freedom of religion includes protection against the government imposing or prohibiting forms of worship. These are called *immunities*. This analysis was first offered in Hohfeld (1919).

3   Criminal law cases in the US are titled "*The People vs. … ,*" indicating that wrongdoers are being prosecuted by the government on behalf of society at large.

4   Hume also adds a third condition: stuff is transferable, so that it is possible to take from others to serve our own needs.

5   Questions: Are there just and unjust ways of resolving this conflict? Is there a difference between fighting over the raft and flipping a coin? And if there are just and unjust ways of resolving it, does Hume's point still go through?

6 Note the stark contrast with Hobbes' theory, according to which justice isn't possible without the enforcement capacity of a strong state.

7 In a celebrated article, Thomson used this idea to defend the right of women to have an abortion. She uses the following thought experiment. Suppose you wake up one day to find some famous violinist hooked up to your body with tubes. You're told that this violinist has some rare disease and needs to be hooked up to you for nine months in order to survive. If you decide to unhook, you are denying that person the opportunity to live their life. But you wouldn't be doing anything wrong. Thomson sees an analogy with abortion: even if the fetus is fully considered a person with a right to life, pregnant women still may choose to abort. So strong are rights over our bodies (Thomson 1971).

8 Rawls' full statement contains some technical terms, as well as additional clauses that have to do with other parts of his theory. I leave those out to avoid complication. The main appeal of the theory is captured by these two principles. The full statement is found in Rawls (1999 [1971]: 266).

9 For the evidence behind this claim, see Van der Vossen and Brennan (2018: 10–16).

10 A related criticism of Rawls' Difference Principle is Nozick (2003 [1974]: 189–97).

11 Mill added that these are protections, the breach of which creates a desire for punishment.

ACTIVISM AND PHILOSOPHY

This book has covered some of the basics of how to do political philosophy. Doing political philosophy means uncovering the logical structure of arguments and theories, identifying their central ideas, and figuring out whether these are really sound or true. Doing this requires hard work, difficult analysis, a commitment to rigor, and intellectual honesty.

The arguments we consider in political philosophy can challenge deeply held beliefs or views. They can even challenge our identity. You may consider yourself a left-wing or right-wing person. But the arguments you'll encounter may challenge that position fundamentally. (They did for me.) If the best arguments don't support your initial position, the mature reaction is to revise your views. Our ultimate goal as students of political philosophy is to find the truth.

Most books like this focus on how we should do political philosophy. But there's a related question, one that's often ignored: how should we *be* as students of political philosophy? There's a connection. The various things we do in life influence one another, and when we pursue one goal or activity, we may be helping or harming our other goals. Pro athletes don't get to eat lots of candy. Students of philosophy, if they want to be serious at least, may have to forgo some things, too.

DOI: 10.4324/9781003250692-7

This chapter is different from the earlier ones. They offered a critical overview of various existing arguments and theories about important philosophical questions. This chapter, on the other hand, asks you to think about how we should conduct ourselves if we wish to be careful political thinkers. I will suggest that if we're serious about studying political philosophy, we might have to be careful about engaging in political activism. Perhaps we have to avoid it altogether.

As always, your job as a student of political philosophy is to assess this argument, and weigh the evidence for and against the various claims that are made. If you find yourself honestly thinking about this issue, considering openly what your positions should be, you're doing it right.

ACTIVISM AND PHILOSOPHY

Anyone who's spent some time at a university knows that many professors and students fashion themselves as political activists. They actively support political parties, organize and attend political events, donate time and money to political causes, put stickers and posters on their doors and around campus, openly root for one side or the other, and encourage others to do the same.

It's commonly said that this is a good thing – that we *should* be politically active. Partisan activism and affiliation are now often defended as part of civic virtue, the responsibilities we all carry as citizens. The reasons that are offered in support of this idea are various. We're told that partisanship makes us think more carefully about political issues. We're told that it helps us understand that we're only on one side of a larger debate, that we can identify with others as members of a larger movement, and so on. Being an activist is not just a way of being a good citizen, but even of being a good person (Rosenblum 2008).

The point is sometimes said to apply to philosophers in particular. We're told that we cannot appreciate the finer points of political life and political problems without involving ourselves directly in politics. Philosopher–activists are thus seen as a kind of "vanguard" for change. They combine the analytical skills of philosophy with firsthand knowledge of social problems (Ypi 2011).

The strongest version of this view comes from the German philosopher Karl Marx. According to Marx, political activism is the entire point of doing philosophy. As the eleventh and final *Thesis on Feuerbach*, which is printed on his tombstone, reads: "The philosophers have only interpreted the world, in various ways; the point is to change it' (Marx 1975 [1845]).

The general idea here is that activism and political philosophy go hand in hand. We should think about politics in order to better do politics. And being political helps us be better at political philosophy. We should be a member of a political party, go campaigning during elections, make political donations, volunteer in advocacy groups, put up yard signs, promote a political party at dinner parties, and generally root for one side or the other.

Many philosophers follow this recommendation with glee. Several years ago, I attended a philosophy seminar sponsored by the National Endowment for the Humanities during the US presidential election. Over drinks after the seminar had concluded, I asked about people's engagement with the election. Everyone but me had donated to a (Democratic) candidate.

At the same time, philosophy is about seeking the truth. And activism doesn't always feel like a truth-seeking business. Activists have a cause, and they defend that cause for all they're worth. When we're committed like that, we're not always open to hearing the opposing side's views or arguments. Trying to have an honest conversation with an activist about the merits of their cause can feel a little like talking to a sports fan, trying to convince them that their favorite team really isn't the best there is.

There seems to be a tension, then. The goal of philosophy is to seek the truth. The goal of activism is to further one's cause, to make the world a better place (at least as one sees it). Thinking carefully about politics can inspire a commitment to change. And the commitment to change can inspire a desire to think carefully about what would really, truly make things better. But still, becoming strongly committed to a cause seems to make it difficult to be as open-minded as we'd like to be. So, here's the question: can we really both be activists and be serious about seeking the truth?

ACTIVISM AND BIAS

It's no coincidence that talking with activists can feel like talking with sports fans. Psychological studies show that people who are committed to political causes tend to be less open to considering relevant evidence about political issues, often in precisely the same ways that sports fans are about their teams. Political supporters suffer from biases, and biases are detrimental to our ability to seek the truth.

The term bias is often associated with certain kinds of prejudice, the kinds that cause or reflect racist or sexist beliefs and actions. But bias is a more general psychological issue. At its core, we suffer from biases when we adopt beliefs on grounds that have less to do with an honest and rational assessment of the available evidence, and more with what fits well with what we like, already believe, or the framework in which it's presented. Psychologist Daniel Kahneman describes biased thinking as involving a kind of substitution. We use answers to easier questions (which are readily available in our minds) to deal with more difficult questions that we're facing. We like to take shortcuts, and these shortcuts can lead us away from believing what's supported by evidence and rational argument.

Psychologists have studied how politically active people form their beliefs about political issues. The dominant force in belief-formation, they've found, is whether a belief or position is adopted by the party or side with which people identify.

Activists, in other words, mainly support policies not on the basis of their own assessment of the policy's virtues, but based on the position of the group or political party with which they identify. This is substitution at work. Instead of doing the hard work of thinking critically about policy, we use political affiliation to arrive at quick and comfortable answers.

Here's an example. Psychologist Geoffrey Cohen studied how liberal and conservative people reacted to two versions of a welfare policy proposal. One version provided generous benefits, the other stringent benefits. Without other information, liberal participants preferred the generous policy, conservatives the stringent one. So far, so predictable. Cohen then added additional information about whether the policy had been proposed by a Republican or Democrat. He found that this information is the most significant factor determining people's support or opposition. Liberals generally support the generous policy if told that Democrats support it, but support the stringent policy if told the opposite. Conservatives support the generous policy if told that Republicans support it, and the stringent policy if told the opposite. Actual policy content had no significant effect on people's responses. We base our support or opposition to policies primarily on "our" party's position (Cohen 2003).

The bias at work here is often called in-group bias. Our reasoning is strongly sensitive to the social groups to which we think we belong. Instead of thinking for ourselves, we tend to conform to beliefs that we think others in our group hold. We substitute the group's beliefs for doing the hard work of thinking about policies ourselves. There are many other biases that reinforce this effect. If we like the person (politician) who proposes a policy, that makes us more likely to accept it. If changing our mind on something would require that we rethink a bunch of other things, we're less likely to change it. If changing our mind on something would require that we reconsider our identity, who we think we are, we're less likely to change it. And so on.

Political activism engages many of these forms of bias. This is especially true for partisan activists, people who broadly identify as Democrats, Republicans, Labour, Tories, or what have you. Partisan allegiance means seeing oneself as having a side, belonging to a group. And having a side typically becomes an important element of how we see ourselves. To many, being pro-choice means seeing oneself as someone who fights for social justice. And with this come various views on other political issues, such as affirmative action, gun control, campaign finance. Being pro-life is of course very similar. Those who hold pro-life views often also favor fiscal discipline, tighter immigration controls, and so on. Even if you haven't thought carefully about each of these issues, you probably still have a preferred view.

This should be a concern. As a truth-seeker, your views should be based on the relevant available evidence. And one's Republican partisan allegiance, say, is not relevant evidence for supporting tighter immigration controls. That's a question about freedom, human rights, culture, national self-determination, and so on. Instead, what happens is that accepting or rejecting certain ideas becomes psychologically costly in light of our partisan identities. Being a Republican but also favoring more immigration can undermine our sense of self in disruptive and uncomfortable ways. And it may get us into hot water with our friends. Our minds like to avoid that. When Socrates challenged the comfortable beliefs of the citizens of Athens, they responded by sentencing him to death. Our friends won't do that, of course, but we still want to avoid the anticipated discomfort by resisting and rejecting (what should be) compelling arguments.

Of course, we're all biased to some degree, including about politics. Activists aren't any more susceptible to bias than others. It's just that, when it comes to political issues, their activism engages their biases in a stronger manner. Politically active people may well be less biased about other issues, issues that they care less about, than people who are passionate about those things. But when it comes to the questions like abortion, say, pro-choice and pro-life activists have a harder time changing their minds.[1]

REDUCING RISKS

The cost of activism, then, is that we become less sensitive to good arguments and evidence. This is a problem for political thinkers. Insofar as we want to be serious about doing political philosophy, we should try to go where the best arguments take us, even if that means changing our minds. Serious political thinkers should be wary of activism.

Of course, refraining from activism won't free you of bias. We all cling to certain views in the face of compelling evidence or argument. No one is perfect. Perhaps you might wonder, then: is it not better to just admit we're all biased, and move on? But this would be a serious mistake. Sure, we're all biased, that's clearly true. But this doesn't mean we can just move on. More bias is worse and less bias is better, at least if we're serious about seeking the truth. And so, we should do our best to reduce our biases.

Consider an analogy:

> **Laboratory Contamination**
> Clements works in a laboratory. The daily experiments Clements is doing need to run for eight hours straight and require him to be present to record results every three minutes. There's no time to leave and have lunch. Clements knows that the laboratory should remain as free from contaminants as it can be. Yet, around lunchtime, he decides to eat a sandwich in the laboratory while the experiment goes on.

It's clear that Clements is doing something wrong. Eating a sandwich in what should be as clean an environment as it can reasonably be, a place where people are required to wear overcoats and hairnets, is not a good idea. The crumbs could fall and contaminate his experimental setup, and that would make it harder for Clements to find out what's really going on. And finding out what's really going on is the entire point of the experiment. Even though he'll get very hungry, Clements should wait until his experiments are done before he eats.[2]

The example Laboratory Contamination is similar to the situation we're in as students of political philosophy. Clements is trying to find out the truth about his experiments – we're trying to find out the truth about political issues. Clements can do or refrain from doing things (eating his sandwich) that would make it harder for him to find that truth – we can do or refrain from doing things (political activism) that would make it harder for us to find the truth. Eating a sandwich runs the risk of contaminating experiments. Political activism runs the risk of contaminating rational thought about politics.

Two things are notable here. First, Clements waiting until the end of the experiment to eat lunch doesn't mean there are no contaminants in the lab. There will always be contaminants that can interfere with one's experiments, things floating in the air, clothing fibers breaking off, a stray hair falling. The experiment is not going to be perfect. But perfection isn't the point. The point is to reduce the risk of contamination. By eating his sandwich, Clements takes a significant risk of contaminating his experiments. And taking that risk is the problem.

Second, it's relatively easy for Clements to avoid taking this risk. Sure, it's hard to skip lunch every day, but it's not like he'll be starving. If starving was what it took to avoid additional risk of contaminating the experiment, then it may well be worth the risk for Clements to eat a sandwich. Some things just ask too much. But that's not the case here. When we're talking about things that are not very difficult or costly to avoid, and would significantly increase the risk of contamination, we can expect people to avoid those things.

Both things can be said about political activism, too. Not engaging in activism won't make you perfectly unbiased. But that's not the point. It'll help you avoid various biases, and that's reason enough. Second, avoiding activism may not be fun, but it isn't like asking you to avoid eating for an entire week. We can expect people to take some measures in order to become better thinkers, and this seems like one of them.

Here's the argument I'm suggesting:

(1)   Political activism increases the risk of biased thinking about politics.

(2)   If we increase the risk of biased thinking about a topic, we risk becoming worse at seeking the truth about it.

(3)   Therefore, political activism increases the risk of becoming worse at seeking the truth about politics.

(4)   If we're serious about doing something, we should avoid doing things that increase the risk of becoming worse at that thing, at least when doing so is not excessively difficult or costly.

(5)   Therefore, if we're serious about seeking the truth about politics, we should avoid political activism.

The argument depends on the following claims. Premises (1) and (2) state the findings of cognitive psychology discussed above. And (3) follows from those points. Premise (4) is a claim about what it takes to be serious about something, as illustrated by the example of Laboratory Contamination. Together, these claims imply (5), that if we want to think carefully about politics, we should be wary about engaging in politics.

OBJECTIONS

Here are three of the main objections I've heard to this argument.

The first holds that political philosophy is not really about seeking the truth. Sometimes it's said that politics is about preference or power – you want one thing, I want another – and the trick is how to get what we want while getting along with one another. To say that there's a true or just way to organize society is simply a mistake, according to this objection. And if politics is not about truth, then even if activism makes us less sensitive to evidence and argument, there really isn't a problem. We have no use for those anyway.

But this cannot be right. First, saying there's no truth in politics makes it very difficult to understand why one should be engaged in activism at all. If there's no truth about, say, women having a right to an abortion, then why would anyone choose to stand outside a Planned Parenthood waving a sign? If there's no truth, then laws about abortion can't be right or wrong, or even better or worse. All they can be is something you like more or less, a matter of pure personal preference or taste. But that doesn't seem like good reason to spend time and energy supporting an issue. It would be like standing outside an ice cream store, holding signs saying chocolate needs to be banned in favor of vanilla. A complete waste of time.

Second, even if there's no truth in politics, that doesn't mean there's no truth in political philosophy. Perhaps politics is just all about power, and there's no fact of the matter about what's a better or worse way to organize society. But even if that's true, there remain important questions for political philosophy. For one, it would be a truth of political philosophy that there is no truth in politics. And that point raises further interesting and important questions. For example, why is there no truth in politics? Is it because there are no moral truths at all? Or do such moral truths exist but not apply to politics? Is there something special about politics such that truth doesn't apply? And so on.

This book has been discussing things presuming that politics is about more than power or preference. And it really isn't plausible to say that there is no truth to politics. Activists holding up signs don't really think they're expressing a mere personal taste. They think it's wrong for women to be denied (or granted) the right to an abortion. But saying that it's wrong for the law to deny (or grant) this right is to imply that there is, in fact, a truth about the matter. And if there's a truth about the matter, then it's worth seeking it. This objection, therefore, means that all those people are confused about what they're doing. They think they're protesting injustice, but in fact they're just expressing a mere preference. This is implausible.

A second objection points out that historically many great political philosophers were involved in politics. John Stuart Mill served as a Member of the British Parliament; John Locke helped author the Constitution of the Carolinas. For them, thinking about the nature of political life and participating in political life seem to have gone hand in hand. Aren't these some of the most influential and brilliant political thinkers of all time? Surely this shows that you can be politically active and still be a great political philosopher.

Clearly, this is right. It is possible. But the point wasn't that political engagement makes it impossible to be a careful thinker. The point was that such engagement makes you less likely to be a careful thinker. Even if Mill and Locke succeeded in pulling this off, it's still a very difficult thing to achieve. That's enough reason to avoid political activism.

Consider again the example Laboratory Contamination above. It's perfectly possible that Clements would find the truth through his experiments, even if he ate his sandwich in the laboratory. It's even possible that this truth would be a profound, historically important one. But he'd still be making it less likely that he'd find that truth, if he chose to eat his sandwich in the laboratory. When we can easily avoid risking contamination, it seems that we should. Clements should wait to eat because that's what a conscientious scientist does. We should steer clear of activism because that's what a conscientious political thinker does.

None of this means there is no place for activism in the world. Nor should we feel like it's a disappointment that philosophers shouldn't be activists at the same time. All it means is that there's a division of labor here, one that separates two different roles. There are thinkers and doers, and being both at the same time is quite the challenge. We shouldn't (and we don't) expect our activists to dedicate their time to being careful thinkers. We understand that they're primarily occupied with bringing about political change, and dedicating much of their time to philosophy can get in the way of that. We should see political philosophy in the same way. We're primarily occupied with understanding what changes would actually make the world a better place. And we should understand that becoming involved in trying to bring about those changes will likely get in the way of that understanding.

It's worth noting here that political engagement in the time of Locke and Mill was seen rather differently. Today's praise of activism represents a sharp break with history. For much of the history of political thought, partisanship or "factionalism" was seen as incompatible with being a good citizen. We should concern ourselves with the good of society as a whole, not just our side's particular interests or values. James Madison famously warned against the dangers of such social and political divisions in "Federalist No. 10" (Madison 2001 [1788]).

Plato famously argued that only philosophers are fit to govern. He had the same idea in mind. Political rulers should have as their objects justice and the common good, not their particular interests. Plato just thought that philosophers were the most likely people to know what those ideas meant. Anyone else, anyone who didn't know about truth and justice, simply wouldn't have a chance at getting things right (Plato 1968 [375 BCE]).

A final objection is more pressing. The argument above says that we can be expected to avoid activism if it's not too difficult or costly to avoid those things. Might it be said that avoiding activism actually is too costly?

Sometimes people say this for silly reasons, basically because they find their activism too central a part of their life. But that won't do. If you find avoiding activism too difficult because you care so much about it, that doesn't make it okay to engage in it. That would be like saying Clements can eat his sandwich because he loves eating so much. If Clements can't bring himself to wait for lunch, then he probably shouldn't work in a lab. Similarly, if we can't bring ourselves to forgo our activism, we shouldn't "attempt" to be serious political thinkers.

But most of the time, the reasons are more serious. It might be true, for example, that we can achieve important things through political engagement. Perhaps this was true of Mill or Locke, at least in their own eyes, when they served in their governmental roles. And being an activist might even teach us important truths about politics, truths that would be difficult to access in other ways. In those cases, forgoing activism would indeed be costly. It would mean giving up on important parts of progress, political or philosophical. And so, despite all that was said above, perhaps activism would still be okay.

We can face a trade-off, then, between keeping our thinking free from activist contamination, and the (other) benefits that such activism might bring. In those cases we should very carefully weigh the goods against the bads and consider what, on balance, would be the best thing to do. Sometimes, that might mean political activism is acceptable, even when we're continuing to try to be serious philosophical thinkers about the issues involved.

But here, too, caution is in order, for two reasons. First, even when we think we're pursuing good and important things, we might be mistaken. Our activism can be a source of bads, as well as goods. Locke helped draft a Constitution that allowed the evil of slavery to continue in the Carolinas. Perhaps he thought this was the best one could do at the time. Perhaps he was simply oblivious. Perhaps worse. But he likely thought he was doing something good. Nevertheless, if Locke had forgone his political work, the overall outcome of his life's work might have been better overall.

Second, cases in which activism does lead to good are very much the exception. They do happen but, most of the time, any person's individual activism achieves rather little. Serving as a Member of Parliament is one thing. Holding picket signs at a rally is quite another. Even if it's true that a big group of people holding signs at a rally can lead to meaningful change, that doesn't mean you showing up as an individual makes much of a difference. After all, whether or not you show up has only a negligible effect on whether the group shows up. The added value of one more person on the corner holding a sign is very small, typically approaching zero.

More often than not, activism is inspired by a feeling that one has to do *something*, even if that something has very little effect. But that's not enough to overcome the argument above. After all, the contaminating effects on our thinking remain very real. And absent real and tangible benefits, there's no trade-off to consider. We should avoid activism.

This is no call for complacency. We can often do things, important things, that do not involve political activism. Instead of protesting homelessness or inequality, we can volunteer at a soup kitchen or give money to those less fortunate. Such acts will often have meaningful and tangible effects. It makes a real difference to a homeless person to receive shelter for the night. It makes a real difference to a single mom on welfare to receive a $500 Amazon gift card. Knowing that people are attending rallies on their behalf, while not actually receiving tangible help, is much less significant.

POLITICS AND ENGAGEMENT

People who study political philosophy obviously care about politics. That's why we start thinking about these things carefully in the first place. We see problems or issues around us, and we think something should be done about them. Sometimes we may have a distinctive idea about a solution. Sometimes we may not be so sure. Often, we'll encounter people who have different ideas. That's how we begin doing political philosophy.

Unless we care about real political problems, it's hard to care about doing political philosophy carefully. And if we don't care, we can't see what may be the important problems that need careful philosophical analysis. But there's a difference between caring about issues and fully committing oneself to one side or another. When we do the latter, we begin to involve our identities as partisans or activists. That's a transition to a different stance, the stance of someone who has a stake in what the right answer might turn out to be. And that's not a healthy stance for a philosopher.

How exactly to balance caring about issues with a commitment to honest and rational thought is something we must figure out for ourselves. But it is something we should take seriously. Just "being aware" that biases exist does very little to reduce them. One of the most replicable findings in cognitive psychology is the "bias blind spot" – the fact that we can spot other people's biases very well, while remaining oblivious to our own. And smarter people, including people trained in philosophy, are no less susceptible to biases (West, Meserve, and Stanovich 2012). In that sense, philosophy is a way of living. It takes commitment and discipline, not only in terms of attending to our analytical reasoning, but also in terms of our broader stance in life.

QUESTIONS

(1) Philosophy is about seeking the truth. But what if we don't find it? Has it been a waste of our time? Why?

(2) Partisan politics engages lots of our biases. Do you think the same is true for single-issue activism? Does it matter whether the issue is central to partisan politics?

(3) If activism can contaminate our thinking about politics, what other things should we be cautious about?

NOTES

1 A good overview, focusing specifically on politics (and religion), is Haidt (2013).
2 Which is what the actual Clements (a good friend of mine in graduate school) in fact did.

.

GLOSSARY

Anarchism The theory that governmental authority is illegitimate.

Argument An inference or form of reasoning that moves from some statements (called premises) to a further statement (called the conclusion) in such a way that the conclusion's truth is supported or established by the truth of the premises.

Authority The ability to change what is morally or legally allowed or required for others.

Bias The result of mental shortcuts where our minds use a more readily available answer as a substitute for a more difficult or challenging one.

Civil Disobedience Disobedience of the law to protest its content and with the intention to reform it. Such disobedience is done openly, non-violently, and in willing acceptance of punishment.

Conclusion A statement in an argument, the truth of which is supposed to be supported by the truth of the argument's premises.

Consent An action by which one gives to others, explicitly or implicitly, rights or permissions with respect to oneself.

Consent Theory A theory holding that governments have legitimate authority over subjects, and subjects have obligations to obey the law, if and only if those subjects have voluntarily consented to it.

Conventional Rights   Rights (see *Rights*) that are the creation of society or government. (Contrasting with *Natural Rights*.)

Democracy   A form of government in which legislation (direct democracy) or leadership positions (indirect democracy) are based on votes by the citizens.

Equality   A political value holding that all people who are relevantly similar be treated in relevantly similar ways. Process-equality requires that people are subject to the same rules, applied impartially. Outcome-equality requires that people enjoy the same or similar outcomes, along some metric (e.g., income, wealth, opportunity).

Freedom (Negative)   The ability to act as one chooses without interference from others.

Freedom (Positive)   The possibility to act in ways that utilize important opportunities and enable one to take control of one's life.

General Will   Rousseau's idea of a collective will that can exist only in political society and focuses on shared or joint interests.

Hypothesis   A statement that purports to explain a certain phenomenon, the truth of which is in principle testable.

Intuition   Something seeming true or correct upon some degree of reflection but without argument.

Justice   A set of rules denoting right and wrong that are of public concern and, at least in principle, enforceable.

Legitimacy   The rightful possession of political authority, or right to rule.

Liberty   See *Freedom*.

Natural Rights   Rights (see *Rights*) the existence of which does not depend on societal or governmental approval or recognition. (Contrasting with *Conventional Rights*.)

Normativity   A dimension of thought that deals with how things ought to be, not how they in fact are.

Political Naturalism   The theory that political authority and hierarchy are natural parts of life in society.

Political Obligation   A moral obligation to obey the law.

Premise   A statement in an argument the truth of which is supposed to support the truth of the argument's conclusion.

Reflective Equilibrium   A point in our reflection where a balance is struck between initial ideas and plausible principles.

Rights   A concept denoting moral or legal freedoms (such that actions breach no moral or legal obligation), claims (to be fulfilled by others' compliance with obligations), abilities (to change legal or moral rights and obligations), or protections (against having certain rights or obligations altered).

Social Contract   An agreement between the members of society to obey a common set of rules. It can be actual or hypothetical (under suitable reflection and discussion).

State of Nature   A condition in which no government exists.

Theory   A set of statements that combines to purportedly explain or justify a certain phenomenon or range of phenomena.

Thought Experiments   Imaginary situations that help isolate a (moral or political) variable, relevant to understanding a broader moral or political question.

Utilitarianism   An ethical theory that holds that the right thing to do is what maximizes overall happiness.

Voluntarism   The theory that authority must be (in some way) freely accepted in order to be legitimate.

BIBLIOGRAPHY

Anderson, Elizabeth. 1999. "What Is the Point of Equality?" *Ethics* 109 (2): 287–337.

Aristotle. 1999. *Nicomachean Ethics*. Translated by Terence Irwin. 2nd ed. Indianapolis, IN: Hackett Publishing.

Aristotle. 2014. *The Complete Works of Aristotle: The Revised Oxford Translation*. Edited by Jonathan Barnes. Vol. 2. Princeton, NJ: Princeton University Press.

Berlin, Isaiah. 1969. *Four Essays on Liberty*. Oxford: Oxford University Press.

Cohen, G.A. 1989. "On the Currency of Egalitarian Justice." *Ethics* 99 (4): 906–44.

Cohen, G.L. 2003. "Party over Policy: The Dominating Impact of Group Influence on Political Beliefs." *Journal of Personality and Social Psychology* 85 (5): 808–22.

Dworkin, Ronald. 1981a. "What Is Equality? Part 1: Equality of Welfare." *Philosophy & Public Affairs* 10 (3): 185–246.

Dworkin, Ronald. 1981b. "What Is Equality? Part 2: Equality of Resources." *Philosophy & Public Affairs* 10 (4): 283–345.

Gaus, Gerald. 2010. "Coercion, Ownership, and the Redistributive State: Justificatory Liberalism's Classical Tilt." *Social Philosophy and Policy* 27 (1): 233–75. https://doi.org/10.1017/S0265052509990100.

Haidt, Jonathan. 2013. *The Righteous Mind: Why Good People Are Divided by Politics and Religion*. New York: Vintage.

Harsanyi, John. 1975. "Can the Maximin Principle Serve as a Basis for Morality? A Critique of John Rawls's Theory." *The American Political Science Review* 69 (2): 594–606. https://doi.org/10.2307/1959090.

Hobbes, Thomas. 1997 [1651]. *Leviathan*. Edited by Richard E. Flathman and David Johnston. Norton Critical Edition. New York: W.W. Norton.

Hohfeld, Wesley Newcomb. 1919. *Fundamental Legal Conceptions as Applied in Judicial Reasoning*. Edited by Walter Wheeler Cook. New Haven, CT: Yale University Press.

Hume, David. 1978 [1739]. *A Treatise of Human Nature*. Edited by David Fate Norton and Mary J. Norton. Oxford Philosophical Texts. New York: Oxford University Press.

Hume, David. 1987 [1752]. "Of the Original Contract." In *Essays: Moral, Political, and Literary*, edited by Eugene Miller, revised, pp. 465–87. Carmel, IN: Liberty Fund Inc.

Kant, Immanuel. 2017 [1797]. *The Metaphysics of Morals*. Edited by Lara Denis. Translated by Mary Gregor. 2nd ed. Cambridge: Cambridge University Press.

Kavka, Gregory S. 1986. *Hobbesian Moral and Political Theory*. Princeton, NJ: Princeton University Press.

King, Martin Luther. 1963. "Letter from a Birmingham Jail." Available at: https://www.africa.upenn.edu/Articles_Gen/Letter_Birmingham.html.

Klosko, George. 2008. *Political Obligations*. Oxford: Oxford University Press.

Locke, John. 1988 [1689]. *Two Treatises of Government*. Cambridge: Cambridge University Press.

Madison, James. 2001 [1788]. "Federalist No. 10." In *The Federalist*, edited by George W. Carey and James McClellan. Carmel, IN: Liberty Fund.

Marx, Karl. 1975 [1845]. "Theses on Feuerbach." In *Karl Marx, Friedrich Engels: Collected Works*, translated by W. Lough Dutt and C.P. Magill, vol. 5, pp. 3–9. New York: International Publishers.

Mill, John Stuart. 2002 [1861]. *Utilitarianism*. Edited by George Sher. 2nd ed. Indianapolis, IN: Hackett.

Nozick, Robert. 2003 [1974]. *Anarchy, State, and Utopia*. Reprint edition. New York: Basic Books.

Plato. 360 BCE "Crito." Internet Classics Archive. Available at: http://classics.mit.edu/Plato/crito.html (accessed May 12, 2022).

Plato. 1968 [375 BCE]. *The Republic*. Translated by Allan Bloom. New York: Basic Books.

Rawls, John. 1999 [1971]. *A Theory of Justice*. 2nd ed. Cambridge, MA: Belknap Press: An Imprint of Harvard University Press.

Rawls, John. 2005 [1993]. *Political Liberalism*. Expanded ed. New York: Columbia University Press.

Ripstein, Arthur. 2009. *Force and Freedom: Kant's Legal and Political Philosophy*. Cambridge, MA: Harvard University Press.

Rosenblum, Nancy. 2008. *On the Side of the Angels: An Appreciation of Parties and Partisanship*. Princeton, NJ: Princeton University Press.

Rousseau, Jean-Jacques. 1923 [1762]. *The Social Contract and Discourses*. Translated by G.D.H. Cole. London: J.M. Dent and Sons. Available at: https://oll.libertyfund.org/titles/rousseau-the-social-contract-and-discourses.

Sen, Amartya. 1999. *Development as Freedom*. 1st ed. New York: Knopf.

Thomson, Judith Jarvis. 1971. "A Defense of Abortion." *Philosophy and Public Affairs* 1 (1): 47–66.

Thomson, Judith Jarvis. 1990. *The Realm of Rights*. Cambridge, MA: Harvard University Press.

Van der Vossen, Bas. 2021. "Consent to Unjust Institutions." *Legal Theory* 27 (3): 236–51. https://doi.org/10.1017/s1352325221000148.

Van der Vossen, Bas, and Jason Brennan. 2018. *In Defense of Openness: Why Global Freedom Is the Humane Solution to Global Poverty*. Oxford: Oxford University Press.

West, R.F., R.J. Meserve, and K.E. Stanovich. 2012. "Cognitive Sophistication Does Not Attenuate the Bias Blind Spot." *Journal of Personality and Social Psychology* 103 (3): 506–19.

Wollstonecraft, Mary. 2009 [1792]. *A Vindication of the Rights of Woman and A Vindication of the Rights of Men*. Oxford: Oxford University Press.

Ypi, Lea. 2011. *Global Justice and Avant-Garde Political Agency*. Oxford: Oxford University Press.

INDEX

Printed in the United States
by Baker & Taylor Publisher Services